EX LIBRIS IS LATIN AND MEANS "FROM THE LIBRARY OF"

THE WEEK Junior ANNUAL
Making sense of the world
2019

EX LIBRIS

This awesome annual of amazing information belongs to

If you happen to find this brilliant book lying around somewhere, please return it to me (although I won't blame you at all if you decide to take a sneaky peek first). Thanks!

PLEASE RETURN

HERE'S ANNA!

Hello!

We started working on this book back in spring 2018 and spent the summer writing, designing and checking every page to make sure that they were all perfect before the annual was printed in the autumn. That's not all we've been doing in 2018, though. As well as making the weekly magazine, the multi-talented *The Week Junior* team have been out and about, meeting our readers and telling people about what we do. Members of the team have hosted workshops at festivals around the country, visited schools, spoken to students and celebrities, participated in podcasts and radio shows, judged competitions and presented prizes. We even launched a brand new monthly magazine called *Science+Nature*, which we are immensely proud of. I hope your 2018 was just as much fun as ours and that 2019 will be even better!

Anna Bassi

Editor-in-Chief

P.S. If you're opening your annual on Christmas Day – Happy Christmas! We hope you enjoy your gift.

WE'RE REALLY PROUD OF THIS AWARD!

DAN AND STEVIE ARE THE BRAINS BEHIND SCIENCE+NATURE.

VANESSA AND JEMMA WITH SOME THE WEEK JUNIOR FANS AT THE JUST SO FESTIVAL.

THE PERFECT BOOK FOR CURIOUS KIDS

THIS IS THE TEAM THAT MAKE THE MAGAZINE.

HERE'S FELICITY MEETING SOME OF OUR READERS.

On the cover: Alamy, NASA, Nintendo, Getty Images, Red Bull Content Pool, CTMG, Sony Pictures Animation Inc, Universal Studios, Shutterstock, REX Shutterstock, Marvel. In the magazine: Liam Arthur, Christian Caron – Creative Commons A-NC-SA, Barb D'Arpingo/Comedy Wildlife Photo 2016, Ben Daure, The Jane Goodall Institute, the Hubble Heritage Team (STScI/AURA), R. Gendler (for the Hubble Heritage Team), G. Miranda/FUNAI/Survival, Rad Sinyak, Yishul Wei / Netherlands Institute for Neuroscience, Alamy, BBC, Caters News Pictures, Disney, Dreamworks via Paramount Pictures, ESA, Epic Games, Evening Standard/Eyevine, Fox, Getty Images, Denis Klero/Red Bull Content Pool, Madrid Police, Marvel, Marvel Studios, MEGA

Contents

Welcome to *The Week Junior Annual 2019*

Every page is packed with fascinating facts and need-to-know information. Tick off each feature when you've read it.

ROVING REPORTER Send your news, jokes and photos to hello@theweekjunior.co.uk. If they're printed in the magazine you'll win a Roving Reporter badge.

THE WEEK Junior

British Media Awards 2018 PRINT PRODUCT OF THE YEAR 2018
British Media Awards 2017 PRINT PRODUCT OF THE YEAR 2017
British Media Awards 2016 BEST NEW LAUNCH 2016
Talent Awards BEST ART TEAM 2017
British Society of Magazine Editors LAUNCH OF THE YEAR 2016

Editor-in-chief Anna Bassi
Editor Felicity Capon
Features editor Ben Isaacs
Staff writers Stevie Derrick, Huw Poraj-Wilczynski, Ciaran Sneddon, Chloe Ward
Editorial assistant Kaye O'Doherty
Art director Dave Kelsall
Designer Munnoo Malik
Picture editor Rachel Billings
Managing editor Vanessa Harriss
Sub-editor Hugh Porter

Contributors Cate Brown, Elizabeth Carr-Ellis, Lee Gale, Tom Jackson, Austin Mackenzie, Mike Mansfield, Lucy Mason, Clare Murray, Ally Oliver, Kevin Pettman, Johnny Sharp, Giles Sparrow, Simon Ward

Digital Production Manager Nicky Baker
Senior Marketing Manager Jemma Foster
Magbook publisher Dharmesh Mistry
Operations director Robin Ryan
Newstrade director David Barker
Publisher and chief executive, The Week Kerin O'Connor
Chief operating and financial officer Brett Reynolds
Chief executive James Tye
Company founder Felix Dennis

The Week Junior Annual 2019 ISBN 978-1-78106-669-0

Licensing & Syndication
To license this product please contact Carlotta Serantoni at carlotta_serantoni@dennis.co.uk

Liability
Although every care was taken during the production of this annual, the publishers cannot be held responsible for the accuracy of the information or any consequence arising from it. The paper used within this annual is produced from sustainable fibre, manufactured by mills with a valid chain of custody. Printed at Artigraficheboccia, Salerno

Dennis

20 questions

Spend a few minutes filling in the answers to our 20 questions. When you look at your book in years to come, it'll be a great way to help you remember what it was like to be you in 2019.

Start here...

1. My age

2. Today's date

3. Where are you sitting right now?

4. What are you wearing? Describe your outfit and draw a picture, too.

5. What was the last thing you did before doing this?

6. Who was the last person you spoke to?

7. Name the best book you read last year.

8. What is your favourite food?

9. Which film did you most enjoy watching in 2018?

10. What's your favourite song?

11. What would be your superpower?

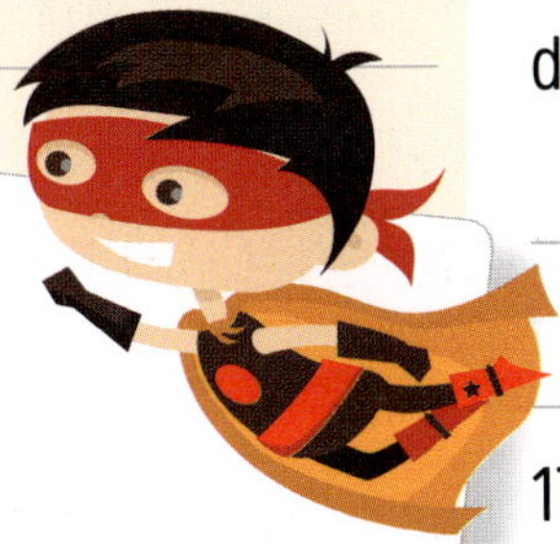

Draw Super You here...

12. What would the book about your life be called?

13. What is the best thing about being you?

14. What's your favourite sandwich filling?

DID YOU KNOW?
The Guinness World Record for the longest line of sandwiches was set on 3 March 2018. The line was just over 4,000 metres long and used 8,100 baguettes, 2,600 kilograms of cheese and 500 litres of mayonnaise.

15. What's your favourite word?

16. What are you going to do in 2019 that you've never done before?

17. What are you most proud of?

18. What makes you happy?

19. Which country would you most like to visit?

WOW!
The origins of the song *Happy Birthday* date back to 1893, when a teacher came up with a tune to greet her class, called *Good Morning to All*.

20. What three things would you like to achieve before your next birthday?

1.

2.

3.

CANADA'S MYSTERIOUS BUBBLING LAKE

Every winter, Lake Abraham in Alberta, Canada, creates a natural spectacle that looks like gems trapped under the ice. These beautiful blobs are frozen bubbles of methane gas, produced by bacteria after they consume dead animals or plants at the bottom of the lake.

AROUND THE WORLD

Turn the page to discover isolated tribes and amazing sights...

UNCONTACTED TRIBES

Uncontacted tribes live in some of the most remote parts of the world.

There are more than 100 uncontacted tribes on Earth. They are groups who do not have any peaceful contact with anyone from the outside world. They live in their own community, with their own language and way of life. These tribes might not have mobile phones or use modern medicines, but they choose to live like this – so it is wrong to refer to them as "lost" or to view their societies as less developed than ours. Some tribes have lived for years in the same way, passing on knowledge about their environment to the next generation. Yet their way of life is under threat as other people battle over the land these tribes call home.

DID YOU KNOW?

One of the most isolated tribes in the world lives on the Andaman Islands off the coast of India. They are called the Sentinelese and very little is known about them.

A distant shot of the Sentinelese.

Where do they live?

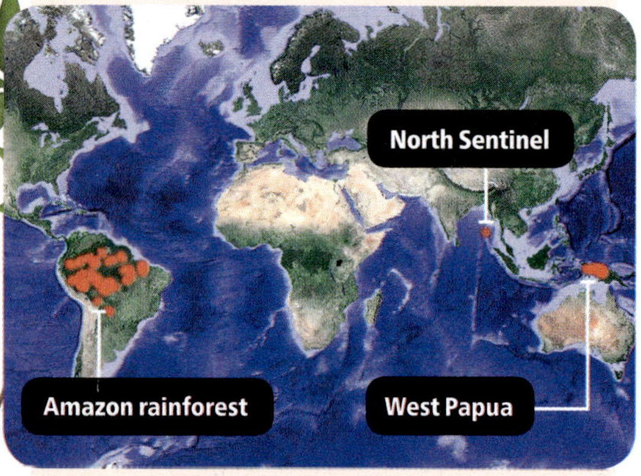

Most of the uncontacted tribes in the world live in the Amazon rainforest, in Brazil, South America. The Amazon is the world's largest rainforest, covering more than 5.2 million square kilometres (that's big enough to fit the UK and Ireland 17 times over). There are also tribes in Asia. The majority of uncontacted tribes live off the land and know a great deal about their surroundings. They know how to hunt and fish, and which berries, fruits and nuts are safe to eat. Since they depend on the environment for their survival, they make sure it is looked after and they do not cause much pollution. They are sometimes called the guardians of biodiversity (a wide range of plants and animals that live together and depend on each other). Some tribes are nomadic, which means they move around and will only stay for a short time in one place. Other tribes are semi-nomadic, so they will stay in a place for bit longer but will also then move on to other locations.

What sort of problems do uncontacted tribes face?

Many tribes are facing difficulties protecting their land. According to Survival International – a charity that supports uncontacted tribes' rights – the problems include logging (when trees are cut down to sell timber), the use of the land to feed animals, mining, oil and gas exploration and road building. The tribes are also at serious risk from disease and illness. Illnesses such as flu or measles can be dangerous for them because they do not have the same resistance to them as you do. When an isolated group has come into contact with outsiders, as much as half the tribe has become ill and died.

The effects of logging.

An uncontacted tribe in Brazil seen from the air in 2010.

Case study: The Yanomami tribe

The Yanomami live in the Amazon.

The Yanomami are a partly uncontacted tribe that lives in the rainforest in northern Brazil and southern Venezuela. They live in large communal houses called yanos or shabonos. The houses are circular and there are up to 400 people in each one. The central area is used for ceremonies, eating and games. The Yanomami believe in equality. They do not recognise chiefs, and decisions are made after long debates in which everybody has a say. The Amazon plays a huge part in their daily lives and the Yanomami use about 500 plants for food, medicine and for house building, among other things. They hunt, fish and grow crops in large gardens. In Yanomami culture, every creature, mountain, rock and tree has a spirit. For more information about uncontacted tribes, go to survivalinternational.org

What does the future hold?

The future is uncertain for uncontacted tribes. The United Nations (a group made up of countries from around the world that addresses issues such as human rights and climate change), introduced a law in 1989 stating that indigenous people (people who have always lived in a certain area, rather than arriving from another country) have a right to live how they choose and that their land should be protected. By raising awareness of the problem, and with support from around the world, it is possible to make sure uncontacted tribes can continue to live according to their customs.

Members of the Yanomami tribe.

Fisherman's friends
A fisherman and his cormorants on the Li River in Guangxi, China.

FISHING WITH BIRDS

Cormorant fishers spend years training their birds to return to the boat with their catch. The birds are given a small fish in exchange for what they've caught.

Nature's fountain
The Fly Geyser in the Black Rock Desert of Nevada, US.

Multicoloured mountain
Rainbow Mountain, or Montaña de Siete Colores, in Peru's Cusco region.

Out in the cold
An elevated dormitory at the Amundsen-Scott South Pole station in Antarctica.

Seeing red
Lake Natron in Tanzania is a patchwork of red water. Minerals flowing into the lake create the colour.

A drop of water
The breathtaking Havasu waterfall on the Havasupai reservation in Arizona, US.

DID YOU KNOW?
Mongolian horsemen may have invented ice cream. One theory suggests the travellers would carry cream in containers and it would freeze in the sub-zero temperatures.

Contacting the ancestors
A shamaness (someone who is believed to communicate with spirits) conducts a ritual in Ulaanbaatar, Mongolia.

THE MOST AMAZING SIGHTS IN THE WORLD

Discover the most spectacular places and events on Earth.

When you think of the greatest wonders of the world, what comes to mind? You might picture Stonehenge in Wiltshire or the Great Pyramid of Giza in Egypt – awe-inspiring buildings or monuments that demonstrate something fascinating about the way humans live. With so many places to choose from, there isn't one official fixed list; there are lots, created by different people and organisations. So we've created *The Week Junior*'s top six sights – places and events you'll want to visit, experience and marvel at.

Building into the sky

Burj Khalifa

The Burj Khalifa towers above other skyscrapers in Dubai, a city in the United Arab Emirates. Almost three times higher than the Eiffel Tower and visible from nearly 60 miles away, at 830 metres it's the tallest building in the world. It houses luxury apartments, hotels, offices and restaurants, and holds seven world records, including the furthest-running lift (which races between more than 160 floors at 10 metres per second).

Mapping the stars

Chichén Itzá

The ancient city of Chichén Itzá in Mexico was once the centre of the Mayan Empire. The Mayans, people native to Central America, were gifted astronomers and used their knowledge of the Sun, Moon and stars to build fabulously complex structures long before the invention of modern technology. The Temple of Kukulkan, part of Chichén Itzá, was built more than 1,000 years ago and has 365 steps, one for each day of the year. On the spring and autumn equinox (the two days in the year day and night when are the same) the shadow of a serpent appears on the temple and seems to slither down the steps as the Sun sets.

STICKY STONES
Mortar used to bind stones on the Great Wall of China was made from sticky rice.

Defending the realm

Great Wall of China

The Great Wall of China runs 13,170 miles – further than London to Beijing, the capital of China, and back. It was built in stages over 2,000 years to keep out China's enemies, but the best-preserved section dates from the Ming dynasty (1368–1644). It is made up of trenches, walls and natural barriers, including hills and rivers. Around one million people died building it, which also makes it the longest cemetery on Earth. Despite what people think, you can't actually see the Great Wall from space with the naked eye – but it's still a spectacular sight.

FILM LOCATION
Iguazú Falls has appeared in lots of films, including the James Bond film *Moonraker*.

Watery wonderland

Iguazú Falls

The Iguazú Falls is made up of 270 waterfalls spanning 1.5 miles, which lead to a spectacular U-shaped waterfall called the Devil's Throat. This marks the border between two South American countries: Argentina and Brazil. Iguazú Falls is one of the biggest waterfalls in the world and is three times the size of Niagara Falls. The cloud of spray given off by the thundering water covers the surrounding rainforest, which is home to many endangered plants and animals.

A spectacular party

Rio de Janeiro Carnival

For one week every year, people pack the streets of Rio de Janeiro in Brazil to enjoy the lively, drumming samba music and dazzling costumes of the Rio de Janeiro Carnival. It celebrates the start of Lent, the 40-day period before Easter, and features hundreds of themed street parties, or *blocos*. The main attraction is the Sambadrome, where local samba schools competing in front of thousands of people show off handmade costumes, lavishly decorated floats and perfectly timed dance steps.

Survival in action

Great migration of the Serengeti and Masai Mara

Every year, more than a million antelope, wildebeest and zebra make a 600-mile journey across the vast plains of the Serengeti and Masai Mara in Kenya and Tanzania, chasing rain clouds in search of fresh grass to graze. Hundreds of thousands are killed along the way by disease, exhaustion and predators like cheetahs, giant crocodiles and lions, which lie in wait. This remarkable migration peaks in July and August and attracts thousands of tourists every year.

FEARLESS PERSONALITY
"I said I could and I would. And I did." Nellie Bly was renowned for her determination.

The adventures of Nellie Bly

She was labelled the best reporter in America, but who exactly was Nellie Bly?

Nellie Bly was a famous journalist who investigated and revealed many injustices (examples of unfairness) in society. Her career began in Pittsburgh, a city in the US state of Pennsylvania, in 1885, but it would eventually take her around the world – including the battlefields of the First World War.

Humble beginnings

Born Elizabeth Jane Cochran, Nellie Bly grew up in a very poor household. At first she wanted to be a teacher, but she was soon forced to give up school because her mother couldn't afford the fees. In 1885, Bly read a newspaper article called "What Girls are Good For", which argued that a woman should always stay in the home, looking after her family. Angered by this, she wrote a strong reply to the editor of the newspaper, *The Pittsburgh Dispatch*. He was so impressed that he gave her a full-time writing job. From then on, she wrote under the pseudonym (a false pen name) Nellie Bly – the title of a popular song at the time.

A life of disguise

Bly's career was now under way, but it wasn't until she moved to New York that she became successful. Here, she went undercover as a patient in a female asylum (a place of care for those with very serious mental-health needs). This required her to pretend to be ill herself, so that she could really experience what it was like.

What Bly discovered there was shocking: filthy conditions; rotten food; and doctors and nurses being violent towards patients. She even found that healthy people were being kept there against their wishes. When her findings were published, the public was outraged. This sparked a bigger investigation, and improvements were made.

Bly's success encouraged her to investigate other wrongs in society and she soon led the way in undercover reporting. She revealed poor working conditions in factories, children abandoned by their parents and corruption (dishonesty) in government.

Female firsts

Proud of her achievement, Bly demanded more money as a reporter. When her boss refused, she quit to work for herself. Bly had often pushed boundaries in this way. She left her first role at *The Pittsburgh Dispatch* because she refused to write about what were then considered to be "women's issues" such as gardening and fashion. Instead, she headed to Mexico, where her criticism of the government led to her being forced out of the country.

Around the world

A newspaper celebrates Bly's achievement.

Despite being a respected journalist, it was an around-the-world adventure that made Bly truly famous. Inspired by a novel called *Around the World in Eighty Days*, written some years earlier, Bly wanted to beat this fictional record – and to write about the experience.

While her boss loved the idea, he wanted a man to go, not Bly. At the time, women were expected to travel with a man for their own protection. Bly, however, was determined. Fearful that she would move to a rival newspaper if he didn't agree, Bly's boss came around to the idea and she set off on 14 November 1889.

Her journey – which involved travelling by boat, train, carriage and horse – took her from England to Egypt, Singapore to Japan. She arrived back in the US 72 days later, beating the fictional record of 80 days.

Bly never lost her adventurous spirit. After many years running her husband's steel company – this eventually failed, causing Bly to lose her fortune – she returned to writing, reporting from the battlefields of Austria during the First World War. As one of America's first female war journalists, she became a role model not only for reporters, but for women everywhere.

Nellie Bly passed away on 27 January 1922, aged 57.

Wordsearch

ANSWERS CAN BE FOUND ON PAGES 94-97

Can you find all of these African countries in the grid? They may be hidden horizontally, vertically or diagonally, and reading either forwards or backwards.

ALGERIA
ANGOLA
BENIN
BOTSWANA
BURKINA FASO
BURUNDI
CAMEROON
CHAD
COMOROS
DJIBOUTI
EGYPT
EQUATORIAL GUINEA
ERITREA
ETHIOPIA
GABON
GAMBIA
GHANA
KENYA
LESOTHO
LIBERIA
LIBYA
MADAGASCAR
MALAWI
MAURITANIA
MOROCCO
MOZAMBIQUE
NAMIBIA
NIGERIA
RWANDA
SENEGAL
SEYCHELLES
SIERRA LEONE
SOMALIA
SOUTH SUDAN
TANZANIA
TOGO
TUNISIA
UGANDA
ZAMBIA
ZIMBABWE

O	C	O	M	O	R	O	S	A	A	N	A	H	G	E	M	E	T	S	T
I	I	M	A	U	R	I	T	A	N	I	A	T	K	L	O	E	Z	B	R
E	I	I	S	I	E	R	R	A	L	E	O	N	E	U	R	U	I	B	D
E	Q	E	A	N	A	W	S	T	O	B	Z	F	R	F	O	Q	D	E	X
A	Q	U	A	E	U	K	L	O	A	E	I	S	I	E	C	I	N	N	M
I	G	D	A	Y	T	A	E	R	A	A	M	E	T	G	C	B	U	I	A
L	R	A	K	T	I	H	U	N	I	I	B	Y	R	Y	O	M	R	N	D
A	S	H	M	B	O	G	I	W	Y	S	A	C	E	P	G	A	U	O	A
M	L	C	I	B	A	R	A	O	L	A	B	H	A	T	A	Z	B	S	G
O	A	M	T	N	I	L	I	L	P	A	W	E	J	T	B	O	Y	O	A
S	A	J	D	O	A	A	T	A	N	I	E	L	P	R	O	M	S	U	S
N	A	A	A	M	G	S	U	G	L	A	A	L	Z	X	N	E	T	T	C
C	Y	Z	L	S	V	O	O	R	A	G	K	E	D	A	N	A	S	H	A
A	B	V	G	R	A	L	B	R	W	R	U	S	A	E	M	A	V	S	R
M	I	S	E	S	A	R	I	Z	I	A	P	I	G	I	S	B	Q	U	L
E	L	G	R	H	G	B	J	U	I	J	N	A	N	Y	R	S	I	D	J
R	P	A	I	I	B	Y	D	O	A	R	L	D	I	E	S	E	Z	A	Q
O	O	S	A	F	A	N	I	K	R	U	B	W	A	Y	A	E	B	N	T
O	S	O	H	T	O	S	E	L	A	I	N	A	Z	N	A	T	P	I	O
N	R	A	I	S	I	N	U	T	D	O	N	I	G	E	R	I	A	S	L

Keyword crossword

Once you have completed the crossword, use the letters in the yellow boxes to spell out another word. Write the keyword in the boxes below the clues.

Across

1 In spite of the fact that (8)
6 Country in Africa whose capital is Cairo (5)
7 Creatures like snails but without shells (5)
9 Still; not emotional (4)
10 Needing to be done straight away (6)
12 Alternative to a bath (6)
14 Performs on stage (4)
17 Teams (5)
18 Large vehicle (5)
19 Trustworthy (8)

Down

2 Faithful (5)
3 Head coverings (4)
4 Not certain (6)
5 Building where people live (5)
6 Reasons not to do something (7)
8 Fulfil a need or desire (7)
11 Ship or boat (6)
13 Command (5)
15 Christmas ___: a song such as *Away in a Manger* (5)
16 Tiny insect (4)

Keyword clue: It has 50 states.

Anagrams

Rearrange the scrambled letters to spell out the names of three currencies.

RUELOB
(CLUE: You'll find this in Russia)

NODUP
(CLUE: Might have the Queen's head on it)

ALLROD
(CLUE: Can be green in colour)

Sudoku

Place the numbers from 1 to 6 exactly once in each row, column and 2x3 bold-lined box, to complete the grid.

	5		4		
				1	5
	3	1			
			1	3	
6	4				
		3		6	

Spot the difference

These two pictures of a performer at Rio Carnival in Brazil might appear to be the same, but take a closer look. There are five fiendishly hard-to-find differences. Can you spot them?

BIG DEBATE

Should everyone learn a second language?

Some people say that learning more than one is a waste of time.

SAY WHAT? There are thought to be more than 7,000 languages spoken around the world.

In a world of air travel and international business, being able to talk to people from other countries is important. In the UK, many schoolchildren learn a second language at primary school and for at least a few years at secondary school – it could be Chinese, French, Spanish or something else. This isn't just good for talking to people from different countries and making new friends; scientists have observed that learning a new language can boost our brain power, too. Learning a new language has also been shown to improve memory, the ability to multitask, and decision making. Yet researchers say that English is currently the third most widely spoken language in the world – with 1.5 billion speakers – so is there any point in learning another one? Besides, lots of people find learning a new language difficult, so is there any need?

YES

- Speaking another language means you can communicate with local people on holiday and learn about their culture.
- Learning another language is good for you – it has been shown to boost brain power and improve memory.
- Speaking a second language makes it easier to study and work abroad. It could also help you get a good job.
- The UK needs people to learn foreign languages so they can do business deals with lots of different countries.

NO

- So many people around the world speak English that there's no need to learn another language.
- New technology does the translation for you and helps you to communicate with people who do not speak English.
- Not everyone is good at learning languages – some people might find the experience frustrating and stressful.
- There are plenty of jobs that do not require a second language so there is no need for everyone to learn one.

WHAT DO YOU THINK?

How to...

Pack like a professional

These handy tips and tricks will make packing much easier.

If you're going on holiday this year, you're probably pretty excited. This can make it difficult to concentrate when it comes to packing, and you're more likely to forget something.

One good tip is to use the 123456 rule. For a week-long holiday take: one swimsuit, two pairs of shoes, three pairs of trousers or skirts, four tops, five pairs of socks and six pairs of underwear. You can always adjust the list depending on the weather. Take some time, think about what you need, and pack like an expert.

NEAT! If you look at a Norwegian passport under ultraviolet light, the northern lights will appear on the paper.

Top tips

Be ruthless

To begin with, lay everything you think you will need for your holiday out on the bed. Next, eliminate about half of that because it is unlikely that you will actually wear it all.

Roll it, don't fold it

Rolling up clothes saves space and it also reduces wrinkles. You can roll everything from jeans to dresses and bathing suits to underwear. Think about grouping outfits and rolling them together. This saves even more space.

Books are bulky

If you can't leave the house without a good book, then consider taking something digital instead, like an e-reader. A phone or tablet will have a free books app on it and they're a lot lighter than a bulky book.

Stuff it in shoes

Shoes take up a lot of space in your suitcase, so roll up your socks and stick them inside your footwear. That way you will be making use of all the space.

Dress it up

Pack accessories such as belts or hats. This will make an outfit look different even if it isn't, and that way you can pack fewer clothes. They'll fit nicely in any odd spaces.

DID YOU KNOW? The item people are most likely to forget when packing is their phone charger, according to Amazon.

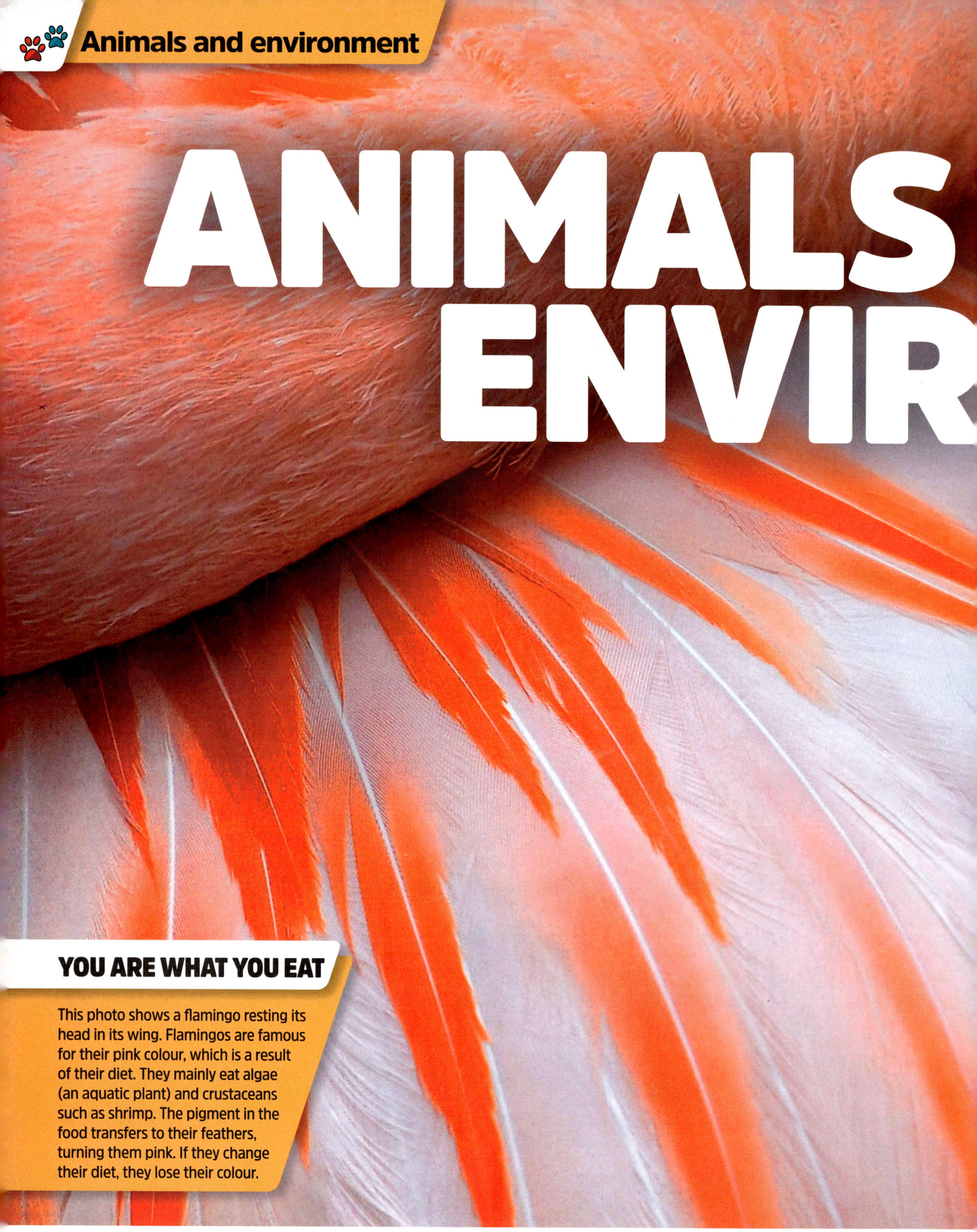

ANIMALS ENVIR

YOU ARE WHAT YOU EAT

This photo shows a flamingo resting its head in its wing. Flamingos are famous for their pink colour, which is a result of their diet. They mainly eat algae (an aquatic plant) and crustaceans such as shrimp. The pigment in the food transfers to their feathers, turning them pink. If they change their diet, they lose their colour.

AND
ONMENT

Meet the champion of chimps, discover our favourite animal heroes and learn all about clouds.

Get your head in

They can block out sunlight and dump buckets of rain on the land, but what exactly are those fluffy things in the sky?

Clouds are made up of water droplets or ice crystals suspended in the Earth's atmosphere (the layer of gases that envelops our planet). Water is around us all the time, but in droplets that are too small to see because they have become a gas called water vapour. Clouds form when damp air gets chilly enough to turn the vapour back into visible water drops or ice crystals.

Clouds are categorised based on their altitude (how far they are away from the ground) and their shape. Each category is given a name based on a Latin word, such as nimbus, which are clouds that bring rain, and stratus, which describe clouds that appear as layers. There are lots of different types of clouds. Here are some of the most eye-catching.

Stratus

This type of cloud can blanket the entire sky, usually close to the planet's surface. When they aren't a complete blanket of cloud, stratus clouds can be horizontally layered. When this type of cloud appears, it tends to be a fairly chilly, dull day.

FAKE CLOUDS

The straight clouds that aeroplanes leave behind aren't really clouds. Known as contrails (short for condensation trails), they are the result of hot air from the plane's engine being cooled quickly by the surrounding air.

Nimbostratus

These are low-level clouds that are full of moisture. Nimbostratus clouds bring continuous precipitation (the term used to describe any form of water falling from the sky, including rain, sleet and snow) that often lasts for hours.

Cumulonimbus

Also known as a thunderhead, this type of cloud produces lots of rain, thunder and lightning. They form when cool air is forced under warm air but they often disappear when the evening arrives and the moisture in the air starts to evaporate.

the clouds

DID YOU KNOW?
Cloud coverage is measured using units known as oktas.

Altocumulus
Described as middle-height clouds, these are patches of clouds (known as cloudlets) that form into rounded clumps. They usually appear during periods of settled weather and can look white or grey.

Cirrus
Found high up in the atmosphere, cirrus are curly, wispy or feathery clouds. Their presence often indicates clear, fair weather and their shape signals which way the wind is blowing.

Cloud mythology

Cloud spirits
According to Greek mythology, clouds were a group of nymphs (young female goddesses who represent things from nature). This group of cloud spirits, called Nephelai, spent their time collecting water from the rivers before floating up to the heavens carrying it in jugs.

Flying elephants
In ancient Hindu tradition, elephants originally had wings and would take flight, showering the land with rain. These winged elephants were described as the clouds of the atmosphere. Airavata, a powerful Hindu god, is the king of the elephants and is said to control the rain clouds.

Clothing for the gods
One of the earliest Native American tribes, the Skidi Pawnee, from the area now found in the US state of Nebraska, believed that clouds were the clothing of the gods. When clouds covered the sky, it meant that a god had spread out his arms, whereas for the early Native American Navajo people, the clouds were formed as a result of a great white swan flapping its wings.

What is pareidolia?

A dolphin appears in the clouds.

Seeing recognisable shapes or patterns in the clouds, such as faces or animals, is known as pareidolia. It is a kind of hallucination (seeing something that's not really there). These types of experiences often reflect the viewer's imagination, and are usually linked to things of interest to that person, whether that's puppies, people or planes. In 2013, a cloud appeared in Essex that people thought looked very like a dolphin.

A corny photo
A cheeky eastern chipmunk tucks in.

Goldilocks
A golden lion tamarin baby clambers around.

Bird watch
A pair of puffins.

Dental inspection
A snail bravely peers into the mouth of a baby crocodile in South Jakarta, Indonesia.

OPEN WIDE
Crocodiles are often seen with their mouths open, like this one. It helps them cool down because they can't sweat. Dogs use the same kind of mouth gaping when they pant.

DEVOTED PARENTS
King penguins don't make a nest for their eggs. Instead, the parents take turns to hold their egg on their feet, switching to the other parent every six to 18 days.

A colony of kings
King penguin chicks stick together in Gold Harbour on South Georgia.

Dragon's den
A weedy seadragon found in coral reefs and off Australia's south coast.

Hold on tight
Two baby common raccoons hang out.

Family lunch
A white rhino mother and its calf graze on the savannah.

ANIMALS TO THE RESCUE

They're smart, loyal and often fearless. Here are some of our favourite hero creatures.

Clever Koko

Koko the gorilla may not have saved anyone's life, but she is still undoubtedly a hero of the animal kingdom. She was loved by millions of people around the world and her death, at the age of 46 in June 2018, prompted global newspaper headlines. She was born in 1971 and was eventually able to understand almost 2,000 words in spoken English and another 1,000 in sign language, which she used to communicate with researchers at The Gorilla Foundation, in the US. She improved conservationists' understanding of gorillas enormously, and made people more determined than ever to protect her species in the wild.

Filippo's flippers

When Davide Ceci, a 14-year-old boy from Manfredonia in southern Italy, fell off his father's boat in the summer of 2000, it seemed likely that he would drown because he had never learned to swim. His father hadn't even realised that Davide had fallen from the boat. Luckily, a friendly dolphin, known to locals as Filippo, came to the rescue. The dolphin pushed Davide back towards the boat and out of the water, allowing his father to pull him to safety.

PRINCESS THE PIGEON

A Second World War medal awarded to a pigeon called Princess raised £8,000 at auction in 2018. Princess was given the medal after flying 500 miles to deliver information to a British base in Egypt.

Ludwig the pig

Ludwig, a pot-bellied pig, is the first of his kind to travel from Canada to the UK to live as a pet. However, that isn't the only reason Ludwig is special. His owners, Mike Maughan and Liane Scholz, came downstairs one morning in 2015 to find someone had broken in and tried to burgle their home, but the sight of Ludwig, who weighs 108 kilograms, had scared them off. His owners said Ludwig makes a noise that "sounds like the biggest Rottweiler you can imagine, so they just ran". Who needs a guard dog when you have a pot-bellied pig?

A helping paw

Poncho practises on a dummy.

Poncho, a Spanish police dog, is no ordinary pup. He is trained in the lifesaving art of cardiopulmonary resuscitation (CPR). CPR is used when someone isn't breathing properly or their heart has stopped. It involves repeatedly pressing up and down on a person's chest and blowing air into their mouth to keep them alive until paramedics turn up. Poncho is trained to jump up and down on a person, pushing his paws on their heart. He also nestles into their neck to check for a pulse – which tells him when their heart has restarted.

Saved by a parrot's squawk

In 2008, a pet parrot called Willie unexpectedly stepped in when his owner's two-year-old daughter Hannah began to choke on a breakfast snack in Colorado in the US. Before then, Willie had only ever been able to copy funny sounds such as kissing, the sound of a dog barking and the occasional word. When he saw Hannah in distress, Willie immediately started squawking very loudly, shrieking, "Mama! Baby! Mama! Baby!" The toddler was saved in time and the family call Willie their "forever hero".

Animals in wartime

Many animals have served armies during times of conflict. Here are just a few.

A statue of Wojtek in Edinburgh.

Wojtek the bear

Wojtek was adopted by Polish soldiers in the Middle East during the Second World War (1939–1945). They took him to Europe and in the 1944 Battle of Monte Cassino in Italy, the bear carried heavy ammunition to soldiers under enemy fire without being injured. He was awarded the rank of corporal, and spent the rest of his days in Edinburgh Zoo.

Sergeant Bill the goat

Canadian soldiers smuggled a goat into France during the First World War (1914–1918). Bill, as they named him, proved he was much more than a mascot by saving at least three soldiers. He head-butted them into trenches, out of the way of exploding shells.

Mali the dog

In 2017, Mali, a British military working dog was awarded the highest award for bravery that can be given to an animal – the Dickin Medal by the People's Dispensary for Sick Animals (PDSA). During his time working for the British Army in Afghanistan, Mali – a Belgian Malinois breed (a bit like an Alsatian) – was sent to search for explosives and alerted soldiers to the presence of the enemy on several occasions.

Goodall in 1965.

DID YOU KNOW?
During a ceremony at Buckingham Palace on 20 February 2004, Goodall was made a Dame of the British Empire.

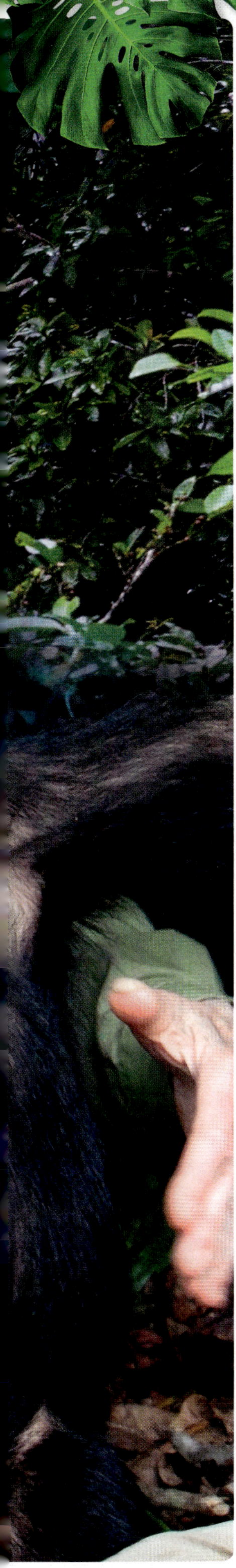

The champion of chimps

Dr Jane Goodall is the only human to have been accepted into a chimpanzee community.

Jane Goodall is one of the most famous primatologists in the world. A primatologist is someone who studies primates – the group of mammals that includes humans, lemurs, lorises and monkeys. Goodall was born in London on 3 April 1934, and her love of animals and Africa began when she was little, thanks to books such as *Tarzan of the Apes* and *The Story of Dr Dolittle*. At 26, Goodall travelled by boat to Tanzania, in Africa, with just a pair of binoculars and a notebook as her equipment. While she was there, she made one of the most incredible discoveries in the animal kingdom.

In the jungle

During her time in the Tanzanian jungle, Goodall took a different approach to that of other primatologists. Instead of numbering the chimpanzees she was studying, she gave them names and began to earn their trust, creating a unique bond and gradually being accepted by the animals as a member of the group. Not only did Goodall disprove the theory that chimpanzees are vegetarians – she observed them eating meat in 1961 – but she also found that it's not only humans who make and use tools. Goodall watched as two chimps, nicknamed David Greybeard and Goliath, used sticks to fish for termites in a termite mound. She strongly believed, and eventually demonstrated, that chimpanzees have emotions and personalities – just like we do.

Roots & Shoots

In 1977, she founded the Jane Goodall Institute for Wildlife Research, Education and Conservation. It's a charity that, among other things, works to preserve chimpanzees and their wild habitats by promoting sustainable living within local communities. Just 14 years later, in 1991, Goodall and 16 Tanzanian students set up Roots & Shoots, which she describes as a "programme for young people in which they decide on projects to improve the world for people, animals and the environment". Funded through donations, tens of thousands of young people across nearly 100 countries have been involved in Roots & Shoots.

An amazing legacy

Goodall has written several books and appeared in lots of wildlife documentaries and TV series to spread her message of protecting chimpanzees and the planet we share with them. She spends much of her year travelling around the world – 300 days on average. She speaks to many different people to raise awareness of the threats chimpanzees face. To find out how you can get involved in Jane Goodall's Roots & Shoots programme, visit rootsnshoots.org.uk

Getting to know Dr Goodall

The Week Junior spoke to the famous primatologist.

What's your greatest achievement?
Since chimpanzees are so like us biologically and because of the equally striking similarities in behaviour and psychology, I was eventually able to help scientists understand that there was not – as I was first taught – a difference in kind between us and other animals. That we were not the only beings with personalities, minds capable of thinking and decision making, and emotions such as happiness, sadness, jealousy and grief.

What is the biggest challenge facing our planet?
Probably climate change, but this is due to other connecting major problems. This includes the unsustainable lifestyles we lead; for example, having far more than we need and depleting finite natural resources at a terrifying rate.

Do you have a particular bond with any animals?
I had a very close bond with a dog called Rusty, who came into my life when I was about 10 years old. I then had a very close relationship with David Greybeard, the first chimpanzee who lost his fear of me, in Gombe, in east Africa [which is now in Tanzania]. He helped me get to know the other members of his community – they were reassured by his calm acceptance of my presence, and gradually they too lost their fear.

Where is your favourite place in the world?
For a long time my favourite place was Gombe. When I could sit quietly, watching the chimpanzees, feeling part of it all. Those were the happiest days of my life, the most meaningful. But it has changed since those early days, with tourists, more infrastructure, more rules and regulations. So now my favourite place is in Bournemouth in the house in which I grew up, which belongs to me and my sister.

Wordsearch

ANSWERS CAN BE FOUND ON PAGES 94-97

Can you find all of these dog breeds in the grid? They may be hidden horizontally, vertically or diagonally, and reading either forwards or backwards.

AFGHAN HOUND
AIDI
AIREDALE TERRIER
AKITA
BARBET
BASENJI
BASSET HOUND
BEAGLE
BERGER PICARD
BLOODHOUND
BOERBOEL
BORDER COLLIE
BORZOI
BOXER
BULLDOG
CHIHUAHUA
CHOW CHOW
ENGLISH FOXHOUND
FRENCH SPANIEL
GOLDEN RETRIEVER
GREAT DANE
GREYHOUND
HAVANESE
LABRADOR
PAPILLON
PEKINGESE
POINTER
POMERANIAN
POODLE
PUG
ROTTWEILER
SALUKI
SAMOYED
SHAR PEI
SHIH TZU
WEIMARANER
WELSH CORGI
WELSH SHEEPDOG
WHIPPET
YORKSHIRE TERRIER

T	Z	E	G	O	D	P	E	E	H	S	H	S	L	E	W	L	T	T	G
R	S	H	A	R	P	E	I	T	E	B	R	A	B	P	W	G	D	Z	C
P	E	A	E	S	H	I	H	T	Z	U	C	L	O	F	G	O	N	G	K
O	E	I	L	L	O	C	R	E	D	R	O	B	R	I	E	L	U	R	N
O	I	I	R	U	E	E	I	T	L	O	P	E	Z	G	N	D	O	Y	A
D	U	N	W	R	K	N	A	J	D	G	N	J	O	R	G	E	H	O	I
L	P	L	H	D	E	I	A	H	N	C	A	A	I	O	L	N	Y	R	N
E	Y	A	I	R	D	T	O	D	H	E	U	E	C	C	I	R	E	K	A
D	H	B	P	I	R	U	E	S	T	H	S	S	B	H	S	E	R	S	R
N	A	R	P	I	N	E	P	L	A	A	C	A	W	S	H	T	G	H	E
U	V	A	E	D	L	A	N	U	A	R	E	O	B	L	F	R	L	I	M
O	A	D	T	O	N	L	H	A	E	D	H	R	B	E	O	I	E	R	O
H	N	O	V	I	B	I	O	L	R	C	E	U	G	W	X	E	O	E	P
T	E	R	E	O	H	S	I	N	W	A	L	R	U	S	H	V	B	T	R
E	S	L	X	C	A	E	M	O	G	L	M	B	I	I	O	E	R	E	E
S	E	E	U	M	W	S	H	U	D	A	T	I	K	A	U	R	E	R	T
S	R	A	O	T	R	C	P	O	R	Q	B	T	E	N	N	S	O	R	N
A	D	Y	T	E	S	E	G	N	I	K	E	P	U	W	D	K	B	I	I
B	E	O	O	S	L	B	E	R	G	E	R	P	I	C	A	R	D	E	O
D	R	U	V	R	O	O	A	F	G	H	A	N	H	O	U	N	D	R	P

Word fill in

All of these environmental words fit in the grid. Can you work out where each word goes to complete it?

4 letters
Soil

5 letters
Green
Ozone
Water

6 letters
Carbon
Energy
Forest
Oxygen

7 letters
Climate
Drought
Recycle

8 letters
Unleaded

9 letters
Renewable
Sanctuary

11 letters
Hydrocarbon

Code riddles

Each of these breeds of cat has had each letter replaced by the letter after it in the alphabet (so A becomes B, B becomes C and so on). Can you break the code to reveal the answers?

QFSTJBO =

TJBNFTF =

SBHEPMM =

Anagrams

Rearrange the scrambled letters to reveal an animal.

HENLEAPT
(CLUE: They have big ears and long noses)

IRONCHORES
(CLUE: They're known for their horns)

APELORD
(CLUE: They're covered in spots)

Number tower

Place a number in every square to complete the number tower. The value in each square is the sum of the numbers in the two squares directly beneath it.

209						
36	50	73	73			
19			40	33		
14		12	21		14	
12	2	3	9	12	7	

Spot the difference

These two pictures of parrots perched on a railing might appear to be the same, but take a closer look. There are five fiendishly hard-to-find differences. Can you spot them?

BIG DEBATE

Should wildlife tourism be banned?

Some people say riding an elephant or swimming with dolphins is cruel.

WHALE... OR DOLPHIN? Orcas, or killer whales as they are often called, are actually dolphins. They are the largest of the dolphin species.

All over the world, thousands of animals are used for wildlife tourism. People travel and pay money to watch monkeys dance and orcas perform stunts, and tourists cuddle tiger cubs and swim with dolphins. It might look like fun, but animal-welfare charities report that in many cases, creatures are suffering. The charity World Animal Protection says that up to 550,000 wild animals are exposed to cruel treatment around the world; in Cambodia, for example, it has been reported that elephants have died from exhaustion after carrying tourists in hot weather. The issue is gaining attention – more than 100 travel companies have already promised that they will no longer promote places where elephants are used for entertainment. However, some people argue that animal tourism isn't always as bad as it seems. So what do you think?

YES

- **Animals weren't put on this planet for our entertainment. They should be free to live as they choose.**
- **The way animals are treated is often cruel and unnatural and causes them suffering. Even if they are treated well, they cannot behave in the same way as they would in the wild.**
- **We don't need these animal attractions. We can see animals close up in their natural habitat in wildlife programmes on the television. There's no need to disturb them in real life.**

NO

- **It is enjoyable and educational for people to interact with these magnificent animals. The more people know about these creatures, the more likely they are to want to protect them.**
- **Wildlife attractions bring money to poor areas and may be the only way for some people to make a living.**
- **Not all creatures at animal attractions are treated badly. Some wildlife attractions protect endangered animals and have breeding programmes that look after rare species.**

WHAT DO YOU THINK?

How to...

Create an ecosystem

An ecosystem is a place where a community of living things, such as animals, bacteria and plants interact with non-living things, like stones and water. Ecosystems are vital; without them there would be no life on Earth. They can range in size from small puddles to huge forests, but it's easy to make your own in a jar and watch what happens.

What you need

- 1 large glass jar with a lid
- Gravel or small stones
- Moss
- Soil
- A small plant that can grow in low light such as a fern
- Ants or worms – but handle them carefully.
- Charcoal (optional). You can buy it online or use a piece of burnt charcoal – when it has cooled – from an open fire or barbecue.

Instructions

1 Place the stones or gravel in the jar. They should cover the base of the jar and be about 2.5 centimetres deep.

2 If using the charcoal, add a few pieces. This will help the jar to stay fresh, but it's not necessary.

3 Find some moss from the park or your garden. Put it in on top of the stones.

4 Add soil on top of the moss. It should fill no more than a third of the jar. You can use potting compost, which you can buy at a garden centre.

5 Next, make a hole in the soil big enough for the plant's roots to fit in.

6 Spray the roots of the plant with water and carefully place it in the hole. You could use a cactus, fern or any small plant. Then fill the hole with soil and lightly water the soil again.

7 Find a few ants and worms or other small creatures from the garden. Place them in the jar – but make sure you handle them carefully.

8 Put the lid on. You can remove the lid once a week to allow in fresh air.

9 Leave the jar somewhere light – but not in direct sunlight – and watch and see how the ecosystem grows and develops.

What will happen?

The plant should grow and you will probably see water form on the inside of the glass. This is water the plant has taken from the soil, converted into energy (to help it grow) and then released. The water goes back into the soil and the cycle continues. The worms and ants will live off nutrients (food) from the plant and in the soil. The plant will refresh the air in the jar by turning carbon dioxide (a gas) into oxygen. The ants and worms do the reverse to the plant – they take in oxygen and release carbon dioxide – so each organism provides something that the other needs. Take notes each week and see how it changes over time.

CIRCLE OF LIFE

Animals eat the plants in the ecosystem, but when the animals die, they decompose (break down) in the soil, which plants then use as food.

Record your observations here:

DID YOU KNOW?

Ecosystems need energy to survive. This usually comes from sunlight, which plants use to turn into energy to grow. This is called photosynthesis.

ASTRONOMICAL DELIGHT

This picture shows spiral galaxy M106. The red wisps are hot gas and the blue specks are dust. These swirl around a black hole at the galaxy's centre, which pulls matter towards it. The image is made up of photos taken in space and from the ground.

SCIENCE & HNOLOGY

Turn the page to take an incredible trip to the Moon.

Fighting the fear

Some phobias are more unusual than others.

What gets you scared? Meeting a giant snake? Finding a tiger in the toilet? It makes perfect sense to be frightened of all these things – the fear keeps you safe. However, some people become very frightened even when there is no real danger. These fears are called phobias, and many types exist. The most common is arachnophobia, the fear of spiders. Less common are anatidaephobia, the fear of being constantly watched by a duck, and sidonglobophobia, the fear of cottonwool balls. These may sound silly, but a phobia sufferer's feelings are very real. Fortunately, doctors are usually able to help patients to overcome their fears.

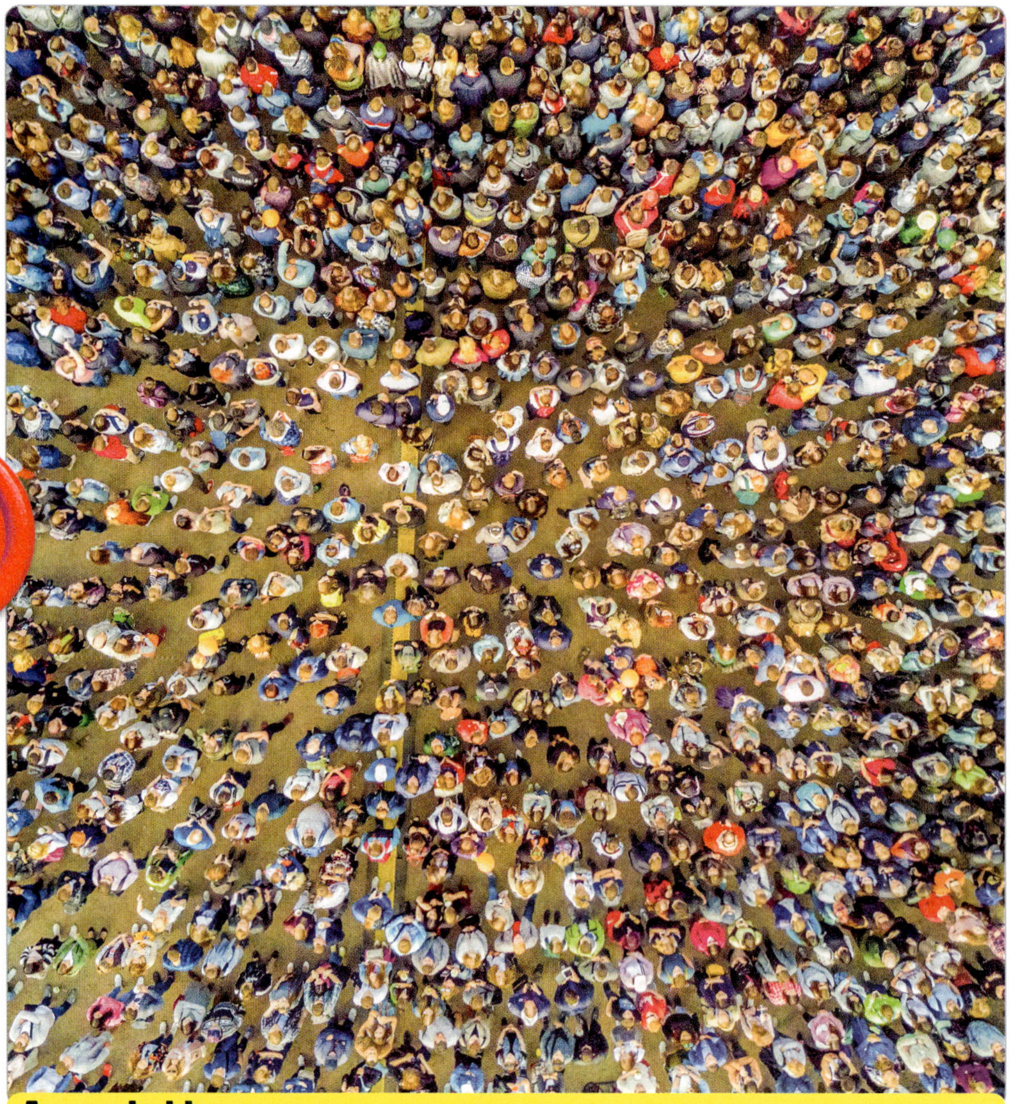

Koumpounophobia

Fear of buttons

This rare phobia leaves people disgusted by the feeling of clothes fastened with buttons – and plastic ones are worse than metal. The phobia leads to sufferers thinking buttons are dirty things covered in germs. Steve Jobs, the co-founder of Apple, was a koumpounophobic, and his dislike of buttons on phones and keyboards is said to be behind the idea of touchscreen devices like the iPad.

Agoraphobia

Fear of crowded places

This common fear affects one in every 150 people. In bad cases agoraphobics feel too anxious to leave their homes. Outside their safe space, sufferers may panic – breathing fast, feeling sick and becoming hot and sweaty. Behaving like this in public, where other people can see them, makes the problem worse, and agoraphobics become scared to enter crowded places. The good news is that most people who seek treatment overcome their fear.

Claustrophobia

Fear of small spaces

One person in 10 suffers from a form of this phobia. Claustrophobics feel trapped when they enter confined spaces, such as lifts, and they may feel faint or have trouble breathing. Sufferers therefore try to avoid these places, but this can make their fear worse. They can, however, be taught to control their anxiety by learning to block out frightening thoughts.

Coulrophobia

NO LAUGHING MATTER

A survey of US adults in 2016 revealed that 42% of them were scared of clowns, but only 32% were concerned about climate change.

Fear of clowns

The clown's red nose, painted face and fixed smile is a well-known sight. We encounter clowns from a very young age at parties or circuses, and although most people enjoy clowns, about 8% of us are scared of them.

Young children, especially before the age of about four, give a lot of attention to faces. A clown's face can look almost normal but not quite right, and the fear could possibly be the result of not understanding what we see.

Pogonophobia

Fear of beards

People with this fear don't react in the same way as those with other phobias. Instead, the fear is a reflection of attitudes towards beards, and the people who have them. It seems many people do not trust a person with a hairy face as much as those who are clean-shaven. The UK's last prime minister with a beard was Lord Salisbury in 1902, and the last bearded US president, Benjamin Harrison, was elected in 1889. Today beards are back in fashion – almost a fifth of British men have one. Are people becoming less suspicious of a bushy face?

Aquaphobia

Fear of water

Deep water is dangerous and unless you're a strong swimmer, you shouldn't venture out too far. Aquaphobics are filled with dread by the idea of water. They worry that they will sink below the surface or that creatures lurk in the dark depths. In extreme cases, panic grabs sufferers whenever they see or touch water – everything from a sea view to taking a bath. The best treatment is to be exposed to water in a safe, relaxed environment, so the sufferer learns to enjoy rather than fear it.

DID YOU KNOW?

Hydrophobia is a fear of water. The word also describes a symptom of rabies – a deadly (but very rare) disease that makes sufferers feel very thirsty but too frightened to drink anything.

WOW!
There are around 30,000 identified species of wasp in the world. Only the females can sting.

Water you doing?
A wasp blows a bubble of water as it works to keep its nest dry.

Walking on air
The Flyboard Air can travel up to 86mph and reach a height of 150 metres.

Flash photo
A performer uses lightning to create music.

Beef beyond belief
Customers at a restaurant in London can pay for their burger by scanning its QR code.

A star is born
A young star, 200,000 times brighter than our Sun, in the Lagoon Nebula.

Rhythm of life
This image represents the activity of a human heart, recorded over 15 minutes.

Sky walker
A NASA astronaut works on the International Space Station.

Flower power
A boy in the Netherlands rides in a solar-powered boat festooned with sunflowers.

DESTINATION: MOON

2019 marks 50 years since the first lunar landing.

On 20 July 1969 (21 July in the UK because of the time difference), Neil Armstrong became the first person to set foot on the Moon. Even 50 years later, the mission is among humanity's greatest technological achievements, but how and why did it happen – and will we ever go back?

DID YOU KNOW? When President Kennedy set NASA the goal of landing a man on the Moon, the US had just 15 minutes of manned spaceflight experience and had not even put an astronaut in Earth's orbit.

The early days

Yuri Gagarin was the first man in space.

The Apollo programme came about because of the "space race" that dominated the 1950s and 1960s. At the time, there was a huge rivalry between the US and the Soviet Union (a country composed of Russia and its neighbours). Both sides used space launches to show their scientific superiority. The Soviets took an early lead, launching the first artificial satellite in 1957 and putting the first man – Yuri Gagarin – in space in 1961. These caught the US by surprise, leaving its space agency, NASA, desperate to catch up.

The plan

President Kennedy inspects a space capsule.

In May 1961, US president John F. Kennedy announced a new goal – NASA would put astronauts on the Moon before the end of the 1960s. Kennedy's aim was to allow the US to catch up and overtake the Soviets. His ambition captured the imagination of the US people and helped justify the programme's enormous cost – the equivalent of more than £150 billion in today's money. The first US astronauts (selected from elite military test pilots – a rule that excluded women) were treated as heroes even before they blasted off.

US president Richard Nixon greets the Apollo astronauts.

Buzz Aldrin walks on the Moon.

The missions

The Apollo 11 Lunar Module.

On 16 July 1969, the three-man crew of Apollo 11 blasted off. They crossed 238,000 miles of space in about three days to orbit the Moon. Two astronauts (Neil Armstrong and Buzz Aldrin) then climbed into the Lunar Module (LM) for descent to the surface, while the third (Michael Collins) stayed in orbit with the main command and service module (CSM). The LM Eagle touched down on the Moon on 20 July, and after several hours, the two astronauts stepped out onto the lunar surface.

The impact

New York City, US, welcomes the Apollo 11 crew.

Apollo 11 marked the climax of the space race and a decisive victory for the US. Five further landings explored the Moon for longer and in increasingly ambitious ways, but the US public was losing interest. After the enormous costs of Apollo, space budgets were cut. However, Apollo forever changed our understanding of the Moon and – by showing Earth as an isolated, vulnerable planet in the vastness of space – it changed our view of Earth itself.

Future Moon missions

Tests take place at NASA's Johnson Space Center.

It seems astonishing that humans haven't yet gone back to the Moon, but NASA's decision to concentrate on working on the reusable space shuttle and then an International Space Station ruled out further exploration of more distant space for a long time. Now, that is finally changing. NASA's new Orion spacecraft, a long-awaited successor to Apollo, will fly its first crewed missions in the early 2020s, with a return to the Moon as one of its first priorities.

WOW! Because the Moon rotates with the Earth, we can only ever see one side of it from the Earth's surface. It wasn't until 1959 that a photo showed us what the other side looks like.

AFTER PARTY

In 2009, Hawking threw a party that was strictly for time travellers and only posted the invitation for the event after it had taken place. Unfortunately, no one turned up.

Scientist of the stars

Hawking guest-starred in *The Simpsons*.

Professor Stephen Hawking changed the way we see the universe.

Stephen Hawking was one the world's most famous and respected scientists. Hawking's groundbreaking work helped us to understand how the universe works and how the world was created. He is regarded as among the most brilliant physicists since Albert Einstein. A physicist is a scientist who studies matter (physical substances) and energy, and the effects they have on each other. He understood more about the universe than most people, and his brilliant theories allowed everyone else to learn more about our world and human existence.

A simple goal

"My goal is simple," Hawking said. "It is a complete understanding of the universe, why it is as it is and why it exists at all." One of his most important ideas involved using the theory of black holes to show that the universe had a beginning. He showed that if there was a Big Bang – the idea that the universe expanded from a single point – it must have started from an infinitely small point, called a singularity. Here time stops and the laws of physics break down.

A new way of thinking

Born in Oxford on 8 January 1942, the eldest of four children, Hawking chose to study physics and maths because they offered the best chance for him to understand the universe. At the age of 21, Hawking was given only a few years to live after being diagnosed with a rare form of motor neurone disease, which is an illness that affects the brain and nerves. This eventually left Hawking in a wheelchair, and he was unable to speak except through a voice synthesiser. Hawking did not let this stop him. Even though he was unable to write, he trained himself to visualise complex problems in his mind. Some of Hawking's co-workers have suggested that this new way of thinking may have helped with his greatest discoveries.

Someone very special

Hawking died on 14 March 2018 aged 76 – more than 50 years after he was told he only had a few years to live. Hawking once said, "We are just an advanced breed of monkeys on a minor planet of a very average star. But we can understand the universe. That makes us something very special." After his death, a memorial service was held for Hawking at Westminster Abbey in London. His ashes were interred (buried) at the abbey and a recording of his voice was beamed into a black hole.

A Brief History of Time

Hawking wanted his theories to be understood by everyone, not just his fellow scientists. He once said that he wanted his "books sold on airport bookstalls". In 1988, he achieved this with *A Brief History of Time*, in which he explains the science of cosmology (the study of how the universe began and how it evolved), including how black holes work. The book explained difficult topics in a way that made them easier to understand. *A Brief History of Time* was a huge success and made Hawking famous around the world. It sold 10 million copies and won a Guinness World Record in 1998 for the longest time a book has been on the bestseller list. He became a celebrity and appeared in episodes of the TV programmes *The Simpsons* and *The Big Bang Theory*. In 2015 a film was released about his life called *The Theory of Everything*. It starred Eddie Redmayne, who described Hawking as "an astonishing scientist, and the funniest man I have ever had the pleasure to meet".

Wordsearch

ANSWERS CAN BE FOUND ON PAGES 94–97

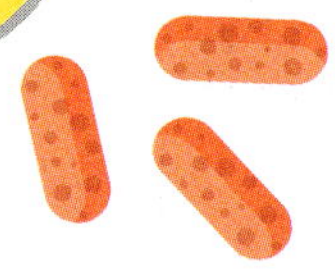

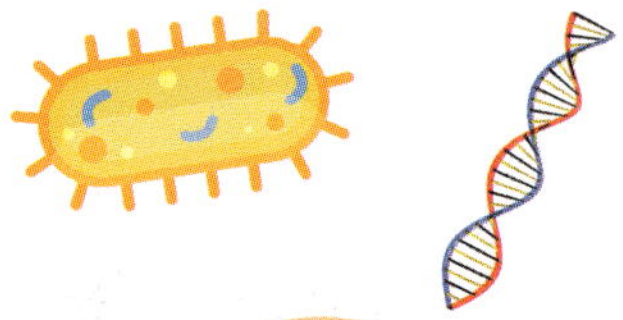

Can you find all of these biological terms in the grid? They may be hidden horizontally, vertically or diagonally, and reading either forwards or backwards.

AMPHIBIAN	DIGESTION	GENETICS	MUSCLES	SIGHT
ANIMALS	DNA	HEART	NOSE	SKELETON
BACTERIA	EARS	HORMONE	NUCLEUS	SKIN
BONES	ENERGY	KIDNEYS	NUTRITION	SMELL
BRAIN	ENZYME	LIFE	ORGAN	STOMACH
BREATHING	EYES	LIVER	PLANTS	TASTE
CARBOHYDRATE	FLOWERS	LUNGS	PROTEIN	TOUCH
CELLS	FUNGUS	MOUTH	RESPIRATION	VIRUS

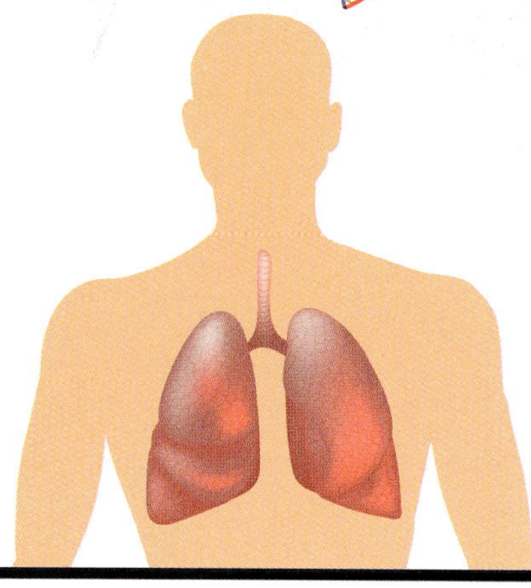

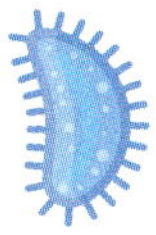

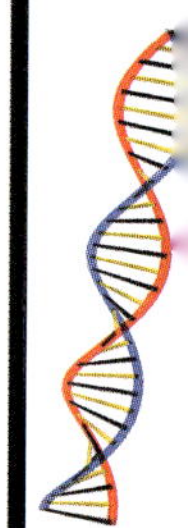

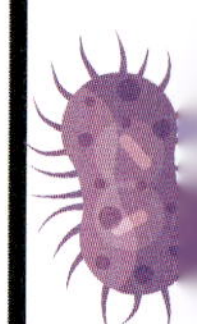

Q	S	L	U	N	G	S	E	O	D	L	C	R	T	O	E	T	S	A	T
P	K	E	F	A	T	F	R	I	V	M	D	G	T	S	V	F	S	M	W
T	I	M	H	U	I	Z	G	L	B	G	N	R	K	P	S	T	U	C	Z
O	N	Y	E	L	R	E	R	H	E	N	A	E	P	R	O	S	A	A	L
N	C	Z	E	R	S	D	P	N	A	E	L	S	A	M	C	R	H	L	O
A	I	N	Y	T	R	G	E	G	H	E	L	E	A	L	B	X	S	T	C
A	Q	E	I	L	J	T	R	U	T	O	K	C	E	O	A	S	U	H	I
I	A	O	B	A	I	O	V	O	S	R	H	S	H	J	Y	T	G	G	H
P	N	D	R	C	E	V	N	S	R	N	N	Y	N	E	Z	N	N	I	C
A	Z	B	S	M	T	Z	E	R	E	L	D	X	N	C	H	A	U	S	U
A	I	R	E	T	C	A	B	R	W	R	A	D	Q	O	T	L	F	N	O
S	S	A	R	E	S	P	I	R	A	T	I	O	N	I	U	P	G	O	T
S	R	X	E	T	F	B	R	T	O	K	T	D	R	S	O	X	I	I	D
U	E	S	S	E	R	O	E	N	A	I	B	I	H	P	M	A	I	T	J
E	W	B	O	N	H	N	Q	A	P	S	S	Q	P	R	O	T	E	I	N
L	O	X	N	O	M	E	H	P	P	L	R	E	N	E	R	G	Y	R	B
C	L	T	W	M	U	S	F	H	L	A	N	I	M	A	L	S	O	T	R
U	F	T	S	R	T	B	R	E	A	T	H	I	N	G	A	T	S	U	A
N	I	T	U	O	D	U	C	G	F	P	S	M	E	L	L	G	I	N	I
A	J	T	O	H	A	Q	S	U	R	I	V	E	Y	E	S	W	U	H	N

Number cross

All of these numbers appear once in the grid below. Can you work out where each of them goes? We've placed one number to start you off.

3 numbers
492
843

5 numbers
16053
17904
23287
28361
34376
55461
64372
65480
72351
~~79811~~

6 numbers
189268
301364

7 numbers
1017646
1338082
3612061
5893754

8 numbers
43008342
87576188

11 numbers
11117406427
11658442486
12832221144
55831155967

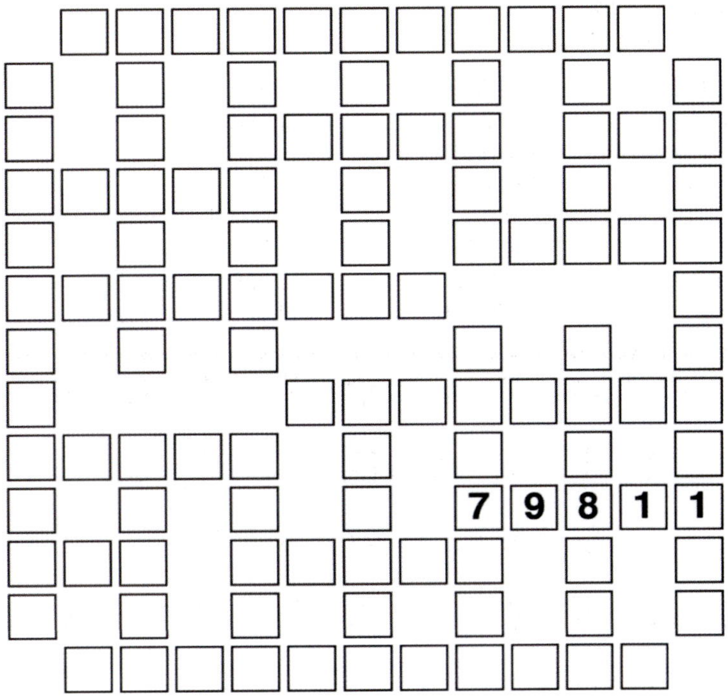

Code riddles

Each of these words relating to chemistry has had each letter replaced by the letter after it in the alphabet (so A becomes B, B becomes C and so on). Can you break the code to reveal the answers?

SFBDUJPO =

PYZHFO =

DIFNJDBM =

WORDFINDER

A word has been hidden in the letter grid on the right. Simply cross out any letter that appears more than once and the hidden word will reveal itself. If you'd like an added challenge, see if you can solve the puzzle in your head without crossing out any letters. Write the hidden word in the boxes below.

Q	P	D	L	R
D	R	O	A	C
J	M	H	X	N
Z	C	Q	J	X
M	H	O	T	Z

Spot the difference

These two pictures of a human and a robot making friends appear to be the same, but take a closer look. There are five cunningly hard-to-find differences. Can you spot them?

BIG DEBATE

Should robots replace human workers?

From serving French fries to exploring space, robots can do all sorts of jobs.

GET TO WORK
The word robot originates from the Cze word *robota*, which means forced work or labour.

Robots are capable of the most incredible things, and they're becoming more and more intelligent. They can clean, cook, work in factories that make cars and machinery, travel into war zones and roam across Mars looking for alien life. Self-driving cars are beginning to appear on the streets and a robot called Atlas, designed by US company Boston Dynamics, is capable of doing backflips. Some robots can care for the elderly. As humans design machines that are smarter and more reliable than ever before, there's a risk that they are beginning to take jobs away from human workers. However, that could be a good thing – robots could end up doing a lot of the boring, difficult or dangerous jobs that humans simply don't want to do, leaving people with plenty more time to think, read, be creative and spend time with friends and family. So should robots replace human workers?

YES

- **Robots are cheaper, more reliable and more productive than human workers. They don't complain, they don't need to be paid wages and they don't need time off for holidays or sickness.**
- **Robots would do the repetitive, boring jobs so that people could do more interesting, creative things. Robots are also good for dangerous work that might put human life at risk.**
- **Throughout history, the way people have worked has always changed. We should embrace technological advances.**

NO

- **If lots of people lose their jobs to robots, they will not be able to make a living and support themselves or their family.**
- **Robots don't have human qualities like empathy and understanding, which are needed in many jobs, such as teaching or nursing. Robots are becoming more creative, but they can't make a piece of art or write a book.**
- **Robots aren't always reliable. Just like computers, they can break down or stop working properly. They can also make mistakes.**

WHAT DO YOU THINK?

How to...

Build a hovercraft balloon

What you need

- The top of a plastic bottle – it needs to be one that you can push in and out
- Strong glue
- An old CD or DVD
- Balloon

Instructions

1 First, wash the bottle lid to ensure it's clean – it must be one that you can push in and out to stop and start the flow of air.

2 Next, cover the bottom edge of the lid with glue, making sure that it has covered the full circumference of the lid.

3 Make sure the lid is in the open position then stick it to the middle of the disc, covering the hole in the centre. Ensure that the lid is stuck on securely and there are no air holes, then set it aside to dry.

4 Once the glue has dried, push the pop-up lid down so that it is in the closed position.

5 Next, blow up the balloon and carefully attach the neck of it to the bottle lid.

6 Place your hovercraft on a smooth surface, such as a table. Open the lid and give it a little nudge to get going.

DID YOU KNOW?
There is a hovercraft museum in Lee-on-Solent in Hampshire.

Make a fizzy volcano

What you need

- A wide-open space outdoors
- Large bottle of fizzy drink
- A packet of Mentos mints
- Safety goggles or glasses

Instructions

Dropping a minty sweet into a bottle of fizzy drink produces seriously explosive results, which is what makes it the perfect make-it-yourself volcano. First, find a wide-open outdoor space to conduct your cool experiment. It can get messy, so you need to make sure you're away from anything that could get damaged. It is also a good idea to wear safety goggles or glasses to protect your eyes from any stray spray. Now all you need to do is take the lid off the bottle and drop three Mentos inside. Now, run! Make sure you're a safe distance away when the bottle erupts in a column of fizzy froth.

WARNING!
Remember to do this experiment outside and stand well back when you drop the Mentos in the bottle.

Record your observations here:

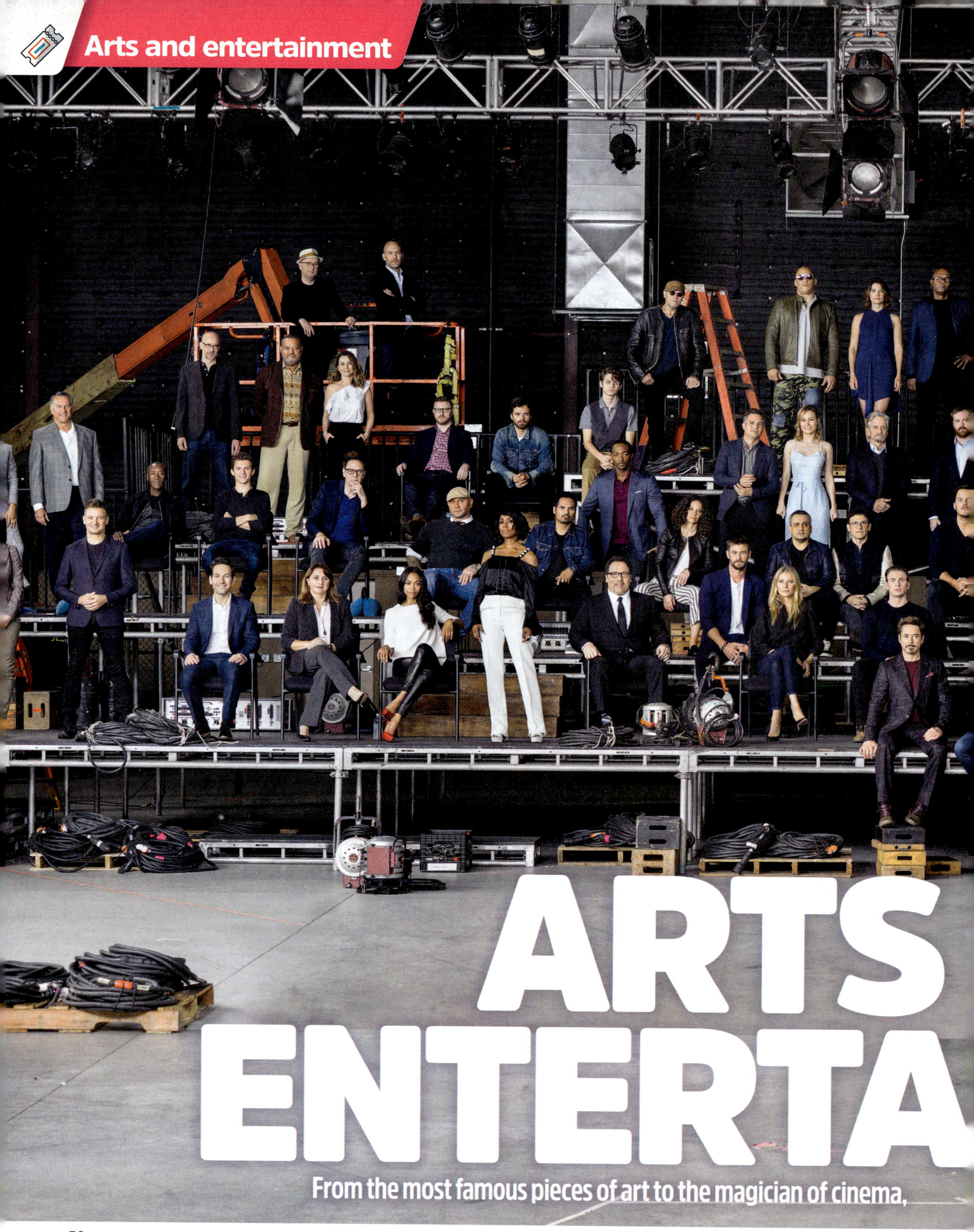

ARTS ENTERTA

From the most famous pieces of art to the magician of cinema,

AS SEEN ON SCREEN

Stars from the Marvel Cinematic Universe celebrate 10 years since the first film in the series, *Iron Man*, was released in 2007. Robert Downey Jr, who plays Iron Man, is front and centre, next to Marvel Studios president Kevin Feige. Chris Evans and Stan Lee, who created many of the characters, sit behind.

AND
INMENT

discover the different ways humans tell stories and express themselves.

A WORLD OF SUPERHEROES

From Spider-Man to Thor, Marvel is home to some of the world's most popular heroes.

For almost 80 years, Marvel has been capturing the imagination of young people and adults with their spectacular superheroes and evil villains. Since its first comic book was published in 1939, Marvel has gone on to produce films, games, TV shows and even theme-park rides that bring its universe to life. Now it is one of the biggest superhero brands in the world.

A heroic history

Marvel's history dates back to 1939, when publisher Martin Goodman created Timely Comics. Timely's first comic release was called Marvel Comics no.1 and was published in October of the same year. The 1940s are often called a golden age of comic books and Timely introduced lots of

superheroes, including Captain America. In 1961, Goodman wanted to create a universe where superheroes interacted like people do in the real world and hired writer Stan Lee and artist Jack Kirby to help. They created Marvel's first superhero team, the Fantastic Four, and Marvel Comics was born. Writer Stan Lee and artist Jack Kirby went on to create the Incredible Hulk, Spider-Man, Iron Man and The X-Men, among others. In all, Marvel has created more than 7,000 characters.

Marvellous Marvel characters

The first issue in 1939.

FIRST SUPERHERO
Marvel's first superhero comic book, *Marvel Comics* no.1 featured a few superheroes in its first issue but the Human Torch is the most recognisable today. In the first comics, the Human Torch was called Jim Hammond, but Stan Lee reinvented the character in 1961, calling him Johnny Storm and making him a member of the Fantastic Four.

BEST TEAM
The Avengers first appeared in the comic book of the same name in 1963. The first Avengers team consisted of Ant-Man, the Hulk, Iron Man, Thor and the Wasp. Now, it includes almost all of the superheroes in the Marvel Universe and is one of the mightiest teams of all time.

MOST POWERFUL HERO
Also known as Carol Danvers and Ms Marvel, Captain Marvel first appeared in the comic book, *Marvel Super-Heroes* no.13, in 1967. Many fans believe she is the most powerful superhero in the Marvel universe. Her powers include durability, flying, strength and the ability to shoot energy bursts from her hands.

The Hulk's power increases when he gets angry.

STRONGEST SUPERHERO
Dr Bruce Banner was turned into the Hulk after he absorbed gamma rays from a bomb explosion. The Hulk has limitless physical strength, which increases with his anger. His power also allows him to jump hundreds of miles at a time and create shock waves when he claps his hands. He first appeared in the *Incredible Hulk* comic books in 1962.

Ultron is made from a special metal.

THE SCARIEST VILLAIN
Ultron is a crazy robot that can think for itself. It was created by fictional scientific genius Dr Henry Pym in the *Avengers* comic books in 1968. Its body is made out of Adamantium, the strongest metal in the Marvel Universe. In the film, *Age of Ultron*, the robot was created by Tony Stark (Iron Man).

DID YOU KNOW?

Marvel created a superhero called Throg in 2009. It was a frog with the same power of Thor.

Marvel in numbers

2,301mph
How fast it is thought that Captain Marvel can fly.

15 years old
The age of Peter Parker, aka Spider-Man, when he was bitten by a radioactive spider.

521 kilograms
The amount Hulk weighs in the comics.

£832,139
How much someone paid for a copy of the *Amazing Fantasy* no.15 comic book. This is Marvel's bestselling comic.

What's next?

Find out about the next Marvel films coming to the big screen.

Behind the scenes of the new *Captain Marvel* film.

CAPTAIN MARVEL
Carol Danvers becomes Captain Marvel to protect the Earth from two alien races who have started a galactic war. The UK release date for Captain Marvel is set for March 2019.

X-MEN: DARK PHOENIX
Based on the life of X-Men's Jean Grey, *Dark Phoenix* tells the story of how Grey's powers began to overwhelm her after the team gets hit by a solar flare. The film is expected to be released in February 2019.

SPIDER-MAN: FAR FROM HOME
The second instalment of *Spider-Man*, starring Tom Holland as Peter Parker, is due for release in July 2019. This time around, Peter heads to Europe with his friends for a summer holiday and meets a villain in the UK.

I-SPY

Legendary comic-book writer and director Stan Lee appears in almost every Marvel film. See if you can spot him next time you watch one.

IRON MAN

The first film released by Marvel Studios was *Iron Man* in 2008. It was chosen because research showed it would be the most popular action figure.

Into the internet
In *Ralph Breaks the Internet: Wreck-It Ralph 2*, Ralph and Vanellope go beyond the arcade.

GET TOGETHER
Lots of characters owned by Disney got together for the *Wreck-It Ralph* sequel, including Moana, Mulan, Elsa, Eeyore, Iron Man and stormtroopers.

Pooh and his crew
Christopher Robin was released in August 2018.

Clowning around
A performer poses at the Venice Carnival.

Perry performs
Katy Perry at the Qudos Bank Arena in Sydney, Australia.

DID YOU KNOW?
Chewbacca was based on creator George Lucas's dog, Indiana, who would often sit in the passenger seat of his car, a bit like a co-pilot.

Stars at sea
Fans dressed as Darth Vader and Chewbacca sail to the Skelligs, in Ireland, for a *Star Wars* festival.

Brighton up your day
Crowds gathered in the sun to watch Brighton Pride 2018.

WORLD OF ART

Six of history's most influential pieces of art

Art is all around us, in the form of drawings, paintings, performances, jewellery, sculptures, videos and more. Throughout history, styles and methods have changed, but many artworks remain popular. Here are six of the most influential and recognisable pieces.

The Starry Night (1889)

Dutch artist Vincent van Gogh is one of the world's most famous artists. Using plenty of paint, lots of colours and short brushstrokes, he depicted beautiful views of the countryside in a style influenced by Impressionism, a technique that involved painting in the open air and working fast to capture the light to create interesting designs.

The Last Supper (1498)

Leonardo da Vinci painted his idea of Jesus's last meal with his 12 closest supporters (the disciples) directly onto the wall of an Italian convent (a building for religious people, usually nuns) over four years. It shows the moment Jesus tells his followers he has been betrayed by one of them, but many people think it also contains secret messages and code about Jesus and his life.

ANCIENT ART
The oldest piece of art ever found is 77,000 years old. Made from ochre (which is found in clay), the carvings feature patterned lines and were discovered in a South African cave.

WOW! The most expensive piece of art ever sold, Leonardo da Vinci's Salvator Mundi, was bought at an auction for £342 million in 2017.

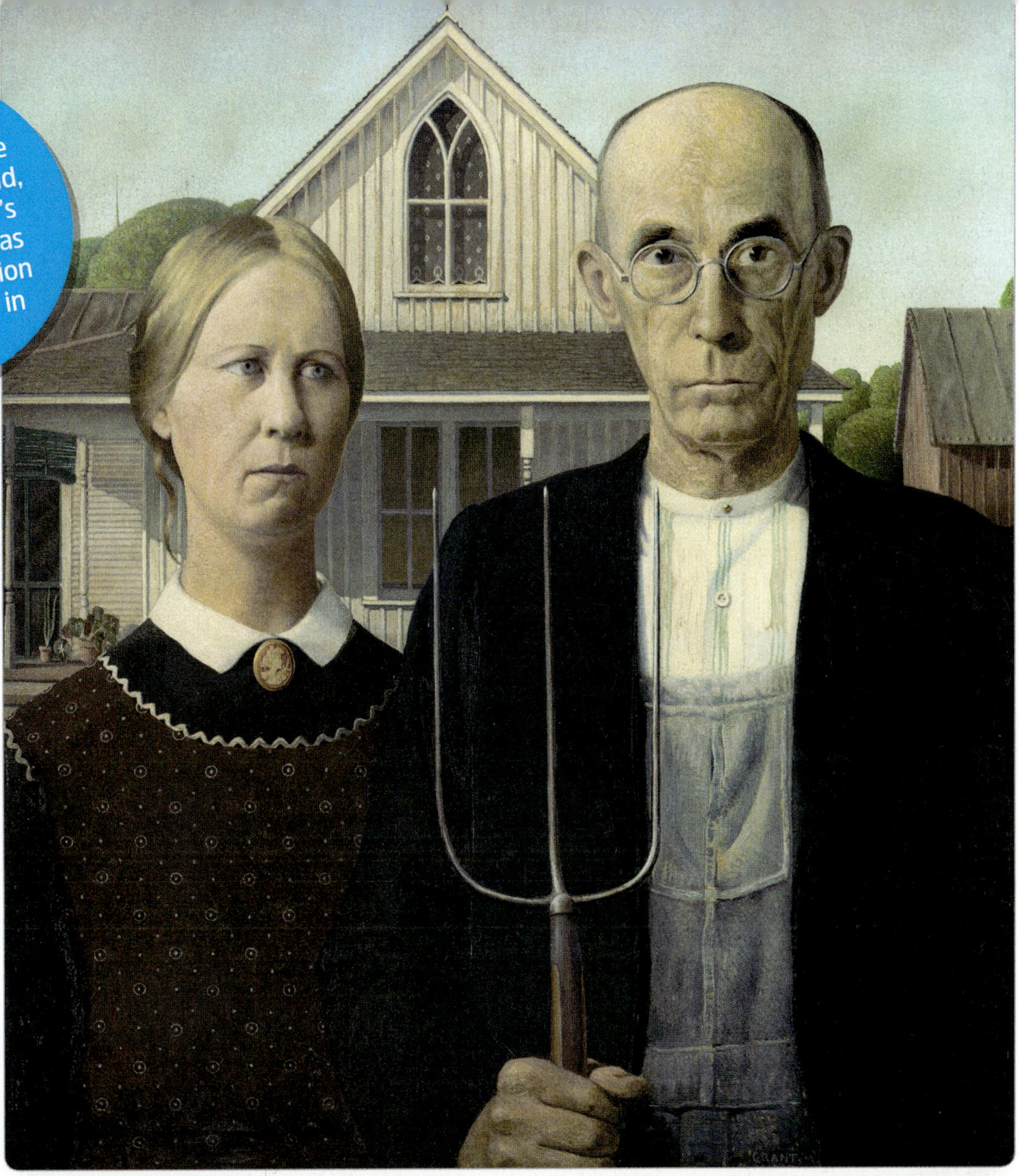

Terracotta Army (around 210BC)

The first leader of China, Shihuangdi, emperor of the Qin dynasty, had an army of around 8,000 life-size clay soldiers built more than 2,000 years ago to protect him in the afterlife. Rulers in the region were typically buried with human sacrifices, but the emperor ordered about 720,000 craftsmen to create the army. It was rediscovered in 1974, and was put on display in Liverpool in 2018.

American Gothic (1930)

During the US's Great Depression (a period of mass unemployment and poverty), this painting by Grant Wood was a sensation. Its gloomy appearance has been described as a portrayal of country life and the pair's strength in tough times. The woman is the artist's sister and the man is a dentist Wood knew. The house behind them is a museum devoted to Wood and the painting itself.

Campbell's Soup Cans (1962)

Campbell's Soup Cans is famous around the world as one of the best examples of Pop Art (artwork that features images of everyday objects). When it was first exhibited in 1962, critics hated it, but it is now well loved. Artist Andy Warhol said he had the soup every day for lunch for 20 years, and the design represents this.

Self-portrait with Two Circles (1665-1669)

In the 1600s (known as the Baroque period), paintings started to look more dramatic and realistic, like this unflattering self-portrait by Rembrandt. Experts disagree on what the circles mean, but most think it's Rembrandt showing off his ability to draw a perfect circle.

WOW!
Famous film director Martin Scorsese paid tribute to Georges Méliès in his 2011 film *Hugo*.

HE SAID IT
"My friends, I address you all tonight as you truly are; wizards, mermaids, travellers, adventurers, magicians... Come and dream with me."

The imagination of Méliès

Georges Méliès was a magician who unlocked the secret of cinema.

Everyone has a favourite film they love to watch, and if yours is a sci-fi film or one packed with lots of special effects, there's a director to whom you owe a special debt of gratitude. No, we're not talking about Steven Spielberg, who made *Jurassic Park* and the *Indiana Jones* films, or George Lucas, the filmmaker behind *Star Wars*. It's a director you might not know, but his contribution to the world of film was out of this world. His name was Georges Méliès, and he changed the way we watch films forever.

Lights, camera, action!

Méliès was a French filmmaker, born in Paris in 1861. After completing his education, Méliès joined his brothers in the family shoe business, where he learnt how to sew. By the 1890s, the very first films were being made. One day, in December 1895, he was invited to an exhibition of the Lumière brothers' invention, the cinematographe. The Lumière brothers were two of the first filmmakers in history. Méliès sat amazed as in front of him pictures moved upon the wall. They were fairly basic scenes from real life but they still had the power to captivate audiences. Méliès, by this time a professional magician, decided he wanted a piece of the action. The Lumières refused to sell him a camera, saying it was "an invention without a future", so he made his own. He didn't just use cameras to record reality, he wanted to make magical motion pictures brimming with special effects.

A studio made from glass

Méliès worked out that he'd need lots of light to make his films, so he set about building a glass-enclosed stage outside Paris in 1897. It is thought to be the first film studio built in Europe. He also constructed almost all of his outfits, props and sets. Méliès was rumoured to have owned more than 20,000 costumes for use in his films. He wrote scripts, designed sets and used actors to film stories. He eventually made more than 500 films, all of which were silent (which means no one talks in them), and many of which starred Méliès himself. In the process he created the first blockbuster in the history of cinema, 1902's *A Trip to the Moon*.

Tricks of the trade

Méliès's background as a magician helped him invent some of the first tricks of the trade. He discovered some of the basic camera tricks which he used to shock his audiences. For example, he would stop the camera, introduce some new props and actors, and then start it up again, creating sudden appearances and disappearances, seemingly from thin air. Another trick made it look as if he were having arguments with himself on screen; elsewhere statues turned into moving people. His films were so popular that they were soon touring the world, and by 1903 Méliès was successful enough to open an office in New York, in the US.

A Trip to the Moon

A rocket lands in the Moon's eye.

In 1902, Méliès made perhaps his most famous film of all time, and one which ensured his place as a legend in the world of film. In the almost 13-minute film, a group of space explorers travel to the Moon, encounter a tribe of strange beings, capture one, and return to Earth. Méliès himself played the crew's leader, Professor Barbenfouillis. The most famous scene shows the rocket launching into the eye of the Moon. You can watch it for yourself at tinyurl.com/TWJ-triptothemoon

The legacy of Méliès

As the first decade of the 20th century drew to a close, other filmmakers started to overtake Méliès with what they could do using the power of film. He eventually lost his business and died in poverty on 21 January 1938 at the age of 76. However, his legacy lived on well beyond his death. One of today's most famous film directors, Martin Scorsese, said that "he invented everything, basically; he invented it all". On 3 May 2018, Google honoured Méliès with its first ever virtual-reality Google Doodle.

Wordsearch

ANSWERS CAN BE FOUND ON PAGES 94–97

Can you find all of the film and book titles in the grid? They may be hidden horizontally, vertically or diagonally, and reading either forwards or backwards.

- A BUG'S LIFE
- ALADDIN
- ALICE IN WONDERLAND
- BRAVE
- CARS
- CHARLOTTE'S WEB
- CINDERELLA
- DESPICABLE ME
- FINDING NEMO
- FROZEN
- HAPPY FEET
- HARRY POTTER
- HOLES
- HOME ALONE
- ICE AGE
- INSIDE OUT
- KUNG FU PANDA
- MADAGASCAR
- MARY POPPINS
- MATILDA
- MINIONS
- PETER PAN
- PINOCCHIO
- SHREK
- TANGLED
- THE BFG
- THE BORROWERS
- THE CAT IN THE HAT
- THE GRUFFALO
- THE HOBBIT
- THE JUNGLE BOOK
- THE LEGO MOVIE
- THE LION KING
- THE WITCHES
- THE WIZARD OF OZ
- TOY STORY
- TREASURE ISLAND
- WALL E
- WINNIE THE POOH
- ZOOTOPIA

S	N	I	P	P	O	P	Y	R	A	M	P	I	N	O	C	C	H	I	O
H	P	N	D	N	A	L	R	E	D	N	O	W	N	I	E	C	I	L	A
R	H	S	F	I	N	D	I	N	G	N	E	M	O	U	U	R	M	S	L
E	O	I	L	G	T	C	I	N	D	E	R	E	L	L	A	T	I	E	A
K	O	D	J	Y	F	A	I	P	O	T	O	O	Z	T	H	A	N	H	D
H	P	E	D	R	H	B	H	T	I	B	B	O	H	E	H	T	I	C	D
K	E	O	N	H	O	T	E	E	N	D	O	R	L	W	H	A	O	T	I
O	H	U	A	I	M	U	H	H	H	K	E	I	C	A	R	S	N	I	N
O	T	T	L	B	E	W	S	E	T	T	O	L	R	A	H	C	S	W	D
B	E	R	S	A	A	I	K	R	L	N	N	R	G	T	C	R	L	E	A
E	I	A	I	B	L	C	W	T	K	E	Y	I	H	N	E	X	S	H	D
L	N	C	E	U	O	E	N	I	E	P	G	E	T	W	A	P	R	T	N
G	N	S	R	G	N	A	N	A	O	E	G	O	O	A	I	T	O	A	A
N	I	A	U	S	E	G	A	T	P	R	F	R	M	C	C	Y	S	D	P
U	W	G	S	L	Z	E	T	E	U	R	R	Y	A	O	S	E	B	L	U
J	Y	A	A	I	O	E	I	F	L	O	E	B	P	T	V	R	H	I	F
E	U	D	E	F	R	L	F	R	B	L	L	T	O	P	A	I	F	T	G
H	E	A	R	E	F	A	S	E	O	E	A	R	E	V	A	T	E	A	N
T	R	M	T	Z	L	C	H	O	M	G	Y	W	E	P	S	H	D	M	U
E	S	E	L	O	H	T	H	E	W	I	Z	A	R	D	O	F	O	Z	K

Keyword crossword

Once you have completed the crossword, use the letters in the yellow boxes to spell out another word. Write the keyword in the boxes below the clues.

Across

1 Particularly; very much (10)
6 Stinging insect (4)
7 The opposite of innocent (6)
8 Round fruits that are red or green (6)
9 Break (4)
11 Type of chair (4)
13 Hate (6)
15 Be present at (6)
17 A rubber ring fitted around the wheel of a vehicle (4)
18 British tennis player (4,6)

Down

2 Product used to clean hair (7)
3 Remove from school (5)
4 Burrows or dens (5)
5 Until now (3)
7 Type of fuel (3)
10 Vienna is the capital of this country (7)
12 Change or alter (5)
13 Father (3)
14 Teacher (5)
16 A popular hot drink (3)

Keyword clue: A funny person.

Sudoku

Place the numbers from 1 to 6 exactly once in each row, column and 3x2 bold-lined box. Can you complete the grid and solve the sudoku puzzle?

6	1		4		
		4			
3		6			
			3		2
			6		
		1		2	3

Anagrams

Rearrange the scrambled letters to reveal a type of entertainer:

ISSOILUNLIT
(CLUE: They perform magic tricks)

ORCAT
(CLUE: They pretend to be other people)

BOATCAR
(CLUE: They're good at gymnastics)

Spot the difference

These two pictures of James Rhodes, better known as War Machine, from *Iron Man 3* might appear to be the same, but take a closer look. There are five fiendishly hard-to-find differences. Can you spot them?

BIG DEBATE

Should snacks be banned from cinemas?

Some people say popcorn and other cinema snacks are a noisy nuisance.

POP!
In 1948, popped kernels around 5,000 years old were found in caves in New Mexico, which suggests that people have been enjoying popcorn for thousands of years.

For lots of people, the experience of taking a seat at the cinema to watch the latest Hollywood blockbuster is incomplete without a big bag or box of snacks and an oversized sugary drink. Whether salty, sweet or a mix of the two, popcorn is a big part of the experience – unless you prefer a hot dog or nachos, of course. For some cinema-goers, however, the sound and smell of other people munching and chewing away can be an unwelcome distraction. Snacks bought in a cinema are usually full of fat and sugar – and they're expensive too. A 2015 study showed that, on average, people spent £7.85 on sweets, popcorn and drinks every time they went to see a film, adding to an already hefty bill for tickets. So, should cinemas crack down on the snackers, or should paying customers be allowed to take whatever they want to eat into the auditorium?

YES

- **Cinemas ask for mobile phones to be turned off, but they allow people to eat nolsy and smelly snacks that are distracting. That's not fair.**
- **Cinema snacks aren't healthy. A large box of salted popcorn at a major UK cinema chain contains more than one third of the recommended daily allowance of calories and fat for adults.**
- **Going to the cinema can already be very expensive, and the cost of snacks is just another way to get money out of paying customers.**

NO

- **Eating popcorn and sweets is part of the experience and adds to the fun of going to the cinema. It wouldn't be the same without these tasty treats.**
- **Selling snacks is an essential way for many cinemas to make money and stay in business. Cinemas also have to hire people to run their food and drink sales. If a ban was introduced, those people would lose their jobs.**
- **There's no reason to ban snacks – they don't hurt anyone. It should be up to individuals to eat what they want.**

WHAT DO YOU THINK?

How to...

Create a photo frame

Most people store their snaps on phones and computers, but making a frame can be a great way to display a special photograph.

What you need

- Scissors
- Thick cardboard
- Ruler
- Pencil
- Paintbrush
- Poster paint
- Glue
- Things to use for decorations such as sequins, coloured paper, buttons, beads or pasta
- Thin card

Instructions

1 Cut a piece of the thick cardboard into a rectangle. Then, using a ruler and a pencil, draw a smaller rectangle in the middle of it and cut it out. The outside portion is your frame.

2 Paint your frame and leave it to dry. Once the frame is dry, you can add the decorations. Stick coloured paper, beads, sequins, buttons and pasta on the frame – whatever you like to make it stand out.

3 Set the frame aside and let the glue dry. Using the thin card, cut a rectangle slightly smaller than the outer frame. This will be the back of the frame.

4 Once the decorations have dried, glue along three sides of the frame and stick the thin card rectangle onto it, leaving one side open so you can slide in your photo.

5 Finally, cut a strip of the thick cardboard and fold the top. Stick the folded part to the back of the frame to help it stand up.

PERSONAL TOUCH

If you are giving the frame to someone as a present, you could customise the decorations to include some of their favourite things.

DID YOU KNOW?

One of the earliest picture frames ever found was discovered in an Egyptian tomb dating back to the second century.

HANDY HINT

Make sure the back of the frame is only slightly smaller than the frame, so you can glue it on.

PICTURE PERFECT

Measure the photo you want to use and make the inside of your frame slightly larger. This way the photo will fit perfectly in the frame.

CAUGHT ON CAMERA

These festival-goers use their phones to capture photos and videos while dancing at a summer party in Crete – an island in the Mediterranean.

ON SCREEN

If you're a fan of video games and addicted to emojis, plunge into the following pages.

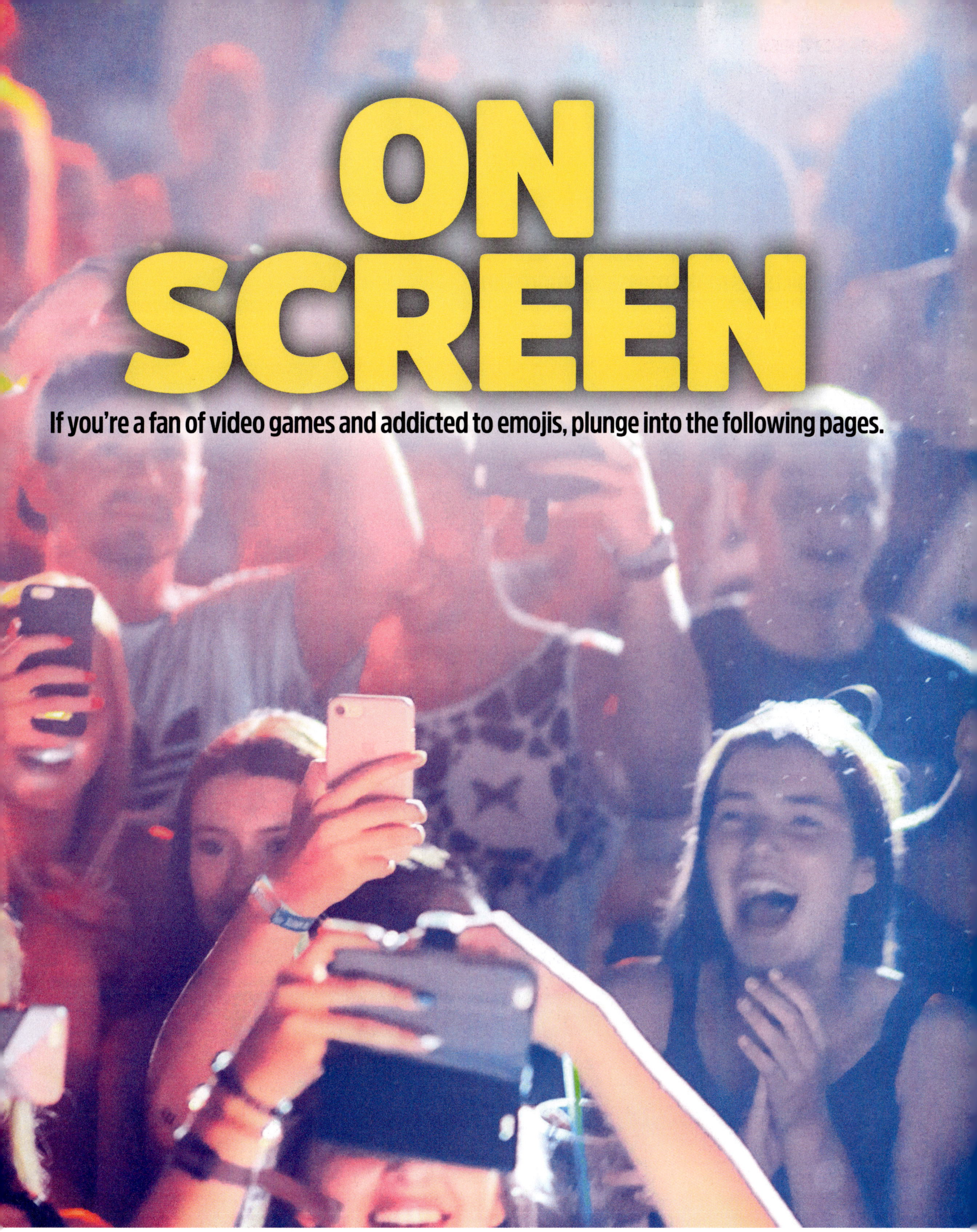

HOW WE FELL IN WITH EMOJIS

The little pictures make messages more fun.

Around 20 billion instant messages are sent every day and emojis are designed to make messages easier to understand. Although the tone of your voice can communicate that you are angry or sad, and a facial expression may show how you are feeling, words on a screen aren't quite so expressive. An emoji – a little character or symbol among the text – is a way of showing an emotion or representing an idea or object.

Early days of emojis

The first emojis were very simple.

At last count there were 2,789 official emojis, These little symbols are fast becoming a visual language that is understood all over the world by people who could never talk face to face. However, this is not why emojis were invented. People have been drawing faces in text for centuries, and in the 1980s, when personal computers and mobile phones were a new thing, people began to use punctuation marks to make mood symbols called emoticons. For example, :-) meant happy and :-(indicated sadness. In 1999, a Japanese designer, Shigetaka Kurita, created 176 symbols to represent simple ideas such as the weather, sport or food. These were the first emojis, but their job was for communicating information in mobile-phone messages, not for helping with the meaning and emotion of those messages. Nevertheless, messaging apps the world over began merging the idea of emojis with emoticons, and in 2010 emoji symbols were included in Unicode (the worldwide code for letters, numbers and other text characters used by all messaging apps).

Emoji evolution

In the 1590s, William Shakespeare wrote "With mirth and laughter let old wrinkles come." In the 1990s, this thought might have been sent by email as "Ha, ha, that was funny!" In a text message sent 10 years after that, it might have read simply "LOL", meaning laugh out loud. Today we just send 😂.

Anyone can request a new emoji, and every week the Unicode Consortium meets to decide what is in – and what is not. New emoji designs of people have to include all skin or hair colours and genders, and other items, such as food, are chosen to have the broadest appeal possible. Many of the original food emojis were Japanese, such as sushi and noodles, but since then a wider range of food items have been added – although there still isn't an emoji for fish and chips.

A new list of emojis is published every year, and Apple, Facebook, Google and the other platforms are gradually making their set of emojis look more or less the same as each other's.

WORD UP!

The *Oxford English Dictionary* included emoji in its 2015 edition, which meant it was officially part of the English language.

BURGER BLOOPER

In 2017, Google had to change its burger emoji for Android phones. The tech giant's original symbol had the cheese under the meat patty, not on top of it. That is just wrong!

GOING OFFLINE

Emojis have leapt off the phone screen into games, advertisements and even the calendar. 17 July is World Emoji Day – because that is the date shown on the emoji for calendar.

Facing the future

Emojis have come a long way, very fast. There has even been a film called *The Emoji Movie* (pictured right). Technology companies are always trying to work out ways to make emojis even better. "Online communication has become more expressive," says Ryan Hoover of Product Hunt, who searches for new trends in the way we use technology. In the future you may be able to customise an emoji to show exactly how you are feeling – and it might even be able to speak in your voice.

Appy days
A gamer in Thailand plays Pokémon Go.

Is this the real life?
A woman tries Vitruvian VR, a virtual-reality simulator.

Digital designs
An exhibition at the V&A museum in London explores how video games have evolved.

WAX HAVEN

Master Chief was the first ever video-game character to be turned into a waxwork in Madame Tussaud's, a visitor attraction full of lifelike wax models.

You can see my Halo

A cosplayer dressed as Master Chief, from the Halo games, at an event in Birmingham.

Strike a pose

Fans get in front of the camera at the E3 Electronic Entertainment Expo in California, US.

Peek-a-boo, Pikachu

A performer at the Pikachu Outbreak event in Kanagawa, Japan in August 2018.

Gaming firsts

Find out more about the first games that shaped the digital world.

The very first video game

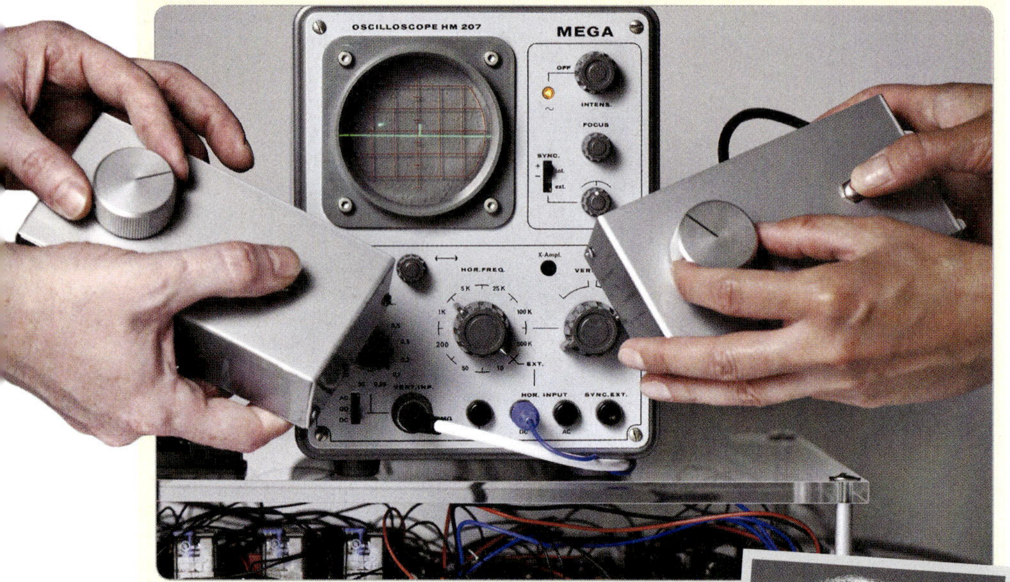

Invented in 1958 by US physicist William Higinbotham, the first video game was a very simple tennis game called Tennis for Two. The game shows a horizontal line, representing a tennis court, with a short vertical line in the middle representing the net. Player one had to hit a button, which sent a virtual ball flying over the net, and player two had to hit another button to send the ball flying back again. The game was extremely popular when it was unveiled at an exhibition in the US in 1958; hundreds of visitors lined up to play it.

The first car-racing game

Many gaming experts think of Gran Trak 10, released in 1974, as the first car-racing video game. Players raced against the clock to complete a course, winning points if they were fast. Gran Trak 10 was an arcade game and used a steering wheel, gear stick, accelerator and brake pedal, so it felt like a real car. It was created by a company called Atari, which went on to make several versions of the game.

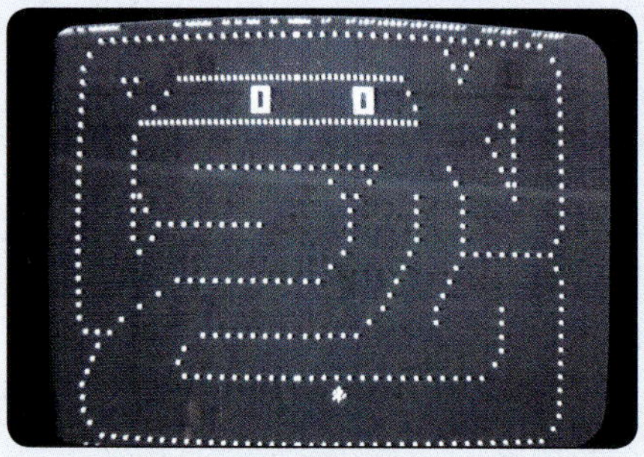

The first arcade game

Developed in 1971 by Nolan Bushnell and Ted Dabney, Computer Space was the first coin-operated arcade video game. Players controlled a rocket and tried to hit two flying saucers. The aim was to score more hits than the enemy spaceships in a set time. Computer Space wasn't as popular as the developers hoped and only 1,500 were sold. However, it did inspire a new era of arcade video games.

OUT OF THIS WORLD

The first game to be played in space was Tetris. It was played by Russian astronaut Aleksandr Serebrov in 1993 on board the Mir space station.

The first 3D game

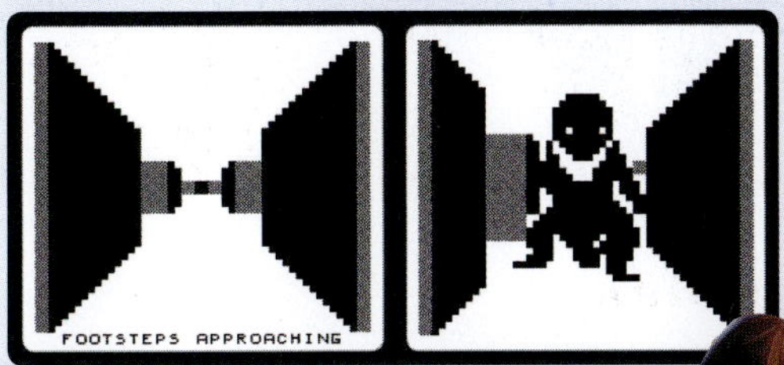

3D Monster Maze was the first 3D-style game for a home computer. It was created in the UK by J.K. Greye and Malcolm Evans in 1981 for the ZX81 computer. Players are put inside a maze and they have to escape, but a ferocious Tyrannosaurus rex is hot on their heels. If the hungry dino finds the player and eats them, the game is over. You can still play it; if you have an iPhone or iPad, you can download a version from the iTunes app store.

PIZZA PAC-MAN

The creator of Pac-Man, Toru Iwatani, said that he thought of the shape of the ghost-munching character while he was eating a slice of pizza.

The first Legend of Zelda game

Nintendo's The Legend of Zelda is an action-adventure game and centres on the playable character Link, who has to rescue Princess Zelda and the kingdom of Hyrule from the evil Ganon. The first in the series was created by Japanese designers Shigeru Miyamoto and Takashi Tezuka and was released in 1986. The newest version of the game was created for Nintendo Switch and Wii U in 2017 and is called The Legend of Zelda: Breath of the Wild. Many gaming critics and fans consider it the best video-game series ever.

The first Mario game

The character of Mario first appeared as Jumpman, the hero in the arcade game Donkey Kong, in July 1981. It wasn't until 1983 that Mario got his own arcade game, called Mario Bros. Mario was created by Japanese game designer Shigeru Miyamoto, who still works for Nintendo. The famous music from 1985's Super Mario Bros is known as Ground Theme and has become one of the most recognisable pieces of game music ever recorded. It has even been performed in concerts by live orchestras.

BEST-SELLING SERIES

Mario and friends have featured in more than 180 games and in 2016 reached a Guinness World Record of 555.35 million sales for Nintendo.

WILD IDEAS
When she was 12, Lovelace had the idea for a flying machine shaped like a horse. A steam engine would power "an immense pair of wings" on the machine to "carry it up into the air while a person sits on its back".

The first computer programmer

Ada Lovelace had a huge influence on modern computing.

On the second Tuesday of October each year, the world remembers the work of the first computer programmer (a person who writes instructions that tell a computer what to do). However, they didn't live in this century, nor even in the last. In fact, the first programmer lived more than 200 years ago.

A child of science

Ada Byron was born in London on 10 December 1815. Her father was Lord Byron, a famous poet who was known for his romantic relationships, scandalous behaviour and great charm.

Her parents split up shortly after she was born and Lovelace never saw her father again. Her mother, Lady Annabella, was determined that her daughter would not grow up like her father, so she kept her away from the poetry and literature that he loved. Instead, Ada learnt mathematics and science. It was unusual for girls at this time to study such subjects, but she showed a great talent for them.

The father of the computer

When she was aged about 17, Ada met the inventor Charles Babbage, who is now known as the father of the computer, and they became great friends. One of Babbage's inventions was the "difference engine", a form of enormous calculator that was turned by a handle. When Ada was able to see an early working model, she was fascinated. She studied and learnt more, becoming an expert in these extraordinary machines.

In 1835, she married William King, the first Earl of Lovelace, and together they had three children. However, she made sure that her marriage would not stop her studies. In a letter to a friend, she wrote, "Matrimony [marriage] has by no means lessened my taste for these pursuits, nor my determination to carry them on".

The Analytical Engine

Her most lasting contribution to computer science came in 1843. She was asked to translate an Italian article about Babbage's latest idea, the Analytical Engine. This was a groundbreaking new machine that could do complicated calculations, store them and print them out. If Babbage had been able to build this incredible device, it would have been the world's first computer.

The text in the article was very complicated and so Lovelace added her own thoughts and ideas to make it clearer. Her notes ended up being three times longer than the original article about the Analytical Engine and covered topics such as looping – where a computer repeats a series of instructions – and writing codes. Her talent and skill meant she could see the potential of the engines to do more than just calculations.

Lasting legacy

It wasn't until computer science really began in the 1940s and 1950s that Lovelace's work was recognised. Her ideas are credited as a major influence on modern computers. Today, computer programmers can write in Ada, a computer language named in her honour, and Ada Lovelace Day is held every year in October to celebrate women in science. In 2017 the Ada Lovelace Institute was opened. It aims to make sure artificial intelligence works for the good of people. So next time you turn on a computer, remember the remarkable woman who helped make the idea come true.

Ahead of her time

Lovelace also discussed artificial intelligence, although she did not believe that machines would ever be able to think for themselves. She even wrote a step-by-step guide describing how the engine could calculate a sequence of numbers. Her guide is now considered to be the first written computer programme. Lovelace predicted that in the future machines could make music, create pictures and help humans with their scientific research.

Sadly, her ideas were very far ahead of her time and far too complicated for most people to understand. As a result, her theories were largely ignored in her lifetime. Ada Lovelace died of cancer on 27 November 1852, in London, and was buried next to her father in Nottingham.

Wordsearch

ANSWERS CAN BE FOUND ON PAGES 94–97

Can you find all of these technological terms in the grid? They may be hidden horizontally, vertically or diagonally, and reading either forwards or backwards.

BACKUP
BLOGS
BOOKMARK
CHATROOM
COOKIE
CURSOR
CYBERSECURITY
DATA
DESKTOP
DOMAIN NAME
DOWNLOADS
EMAIL
FACEBOOK
FIREWALL
FORUM
HARDWARE
HOMEPAGE
ICON
INFORMATION
INTERNET
KEYBOARD
MONITOR
MOUSE
MUSIC
PASSWORD
PICTURES
PRINTER
SCANNER
SEARCH ENGINE
SOCIAL MEDIA
SOFTWARE
SPAM
SURFING
TWITTER
UPLOAD
USERNAME
VIDEO GAMES
VIRUS
WEB BROWSER
WORLD WIDE WEB

Q	K	H	I	C	O	N	C	Z	K	A	P	P	O	T	K	S	E	D	P
U	E	R	P	A	S	S	W	O	R	D	R	L	J	R	C	N	R	Z	R
H	M	B	A	G	J	P	S	E	A	R	C	H	E	N	G	I	N	E	I
F	A	L	R	M	N	F	R	S	P	H	H	T	H	O	B	N	T	N	N
I	N	O	P	S	K	I	R	U	P	L	O	A	D	Y	P	F	C	R	T
R	R	G	I	I	E	O	F	E	I	T	S	U	R	I	V	O	U	A	E
E	E	S	J	H	L	O	O	R	J	F	H	S	D	D	H	R	R	S	R
W	S	B	A	C	K	U	P	B	U	X	A	D	R	R	W	M	S	V	A
A	U	U	Y	T	I	R	U	C	E	S	R	E	B	Y	C	A	O	I	W
L	B	E	W	E	D	I	W	D	L	R	O	W	I	T	S	T	R	D	T
L	T	T	K	W	J	A	B	F	O	R	U	M	T	W	O	I	L	E	F
C	H	A	T	R	O	O	M	B	L	I	H	P	E	S	C	O	O	O	O
K	F	E	M	A	N	N	I	A	M	O	D	B	S	D	I	N	T	G	S
E	A	R	T	R	A	L	L	M	M	A	B	R	E	A	A	R	E	A	C
Y	C	C	O	V	E	R	I	E	U	R	P	O	R	O	L	E	N	M	A
B	E	O	R	T	S	T	P	A	O	S	E	S	U	L	M	S	R	E	N
O	B	O	D	P	I	A	T	W	M	B	I	E	T	N	E	U	E	S	N
A	O	K	A	I	G	N	S	I	O	E	O	C	C	W	D	O	T	G	E
R	O	I	T	E	T	E	O	K	W	L	A	P	I	O	I	M	N	Z	R
D	K	E	A	O	R	B	H	M	N	T	I	R	P	D	A	T	I	R	C

Number cross

All of these numbers appear once in the grid below. Can you work out where each of them goes? We've placed one to start you off.

4 numbers
2586
3293
6689
9808

5 numbers
19559
84986
85890
87041

6 numbers
133956
495479
667808
705627

7 numbers
~~4855468~~
5187235
5751061
9980956

8 numbers
22529877
28583679
44363403
88120467

12 numbers
326302602190
651053096828
681485629581
920530738646

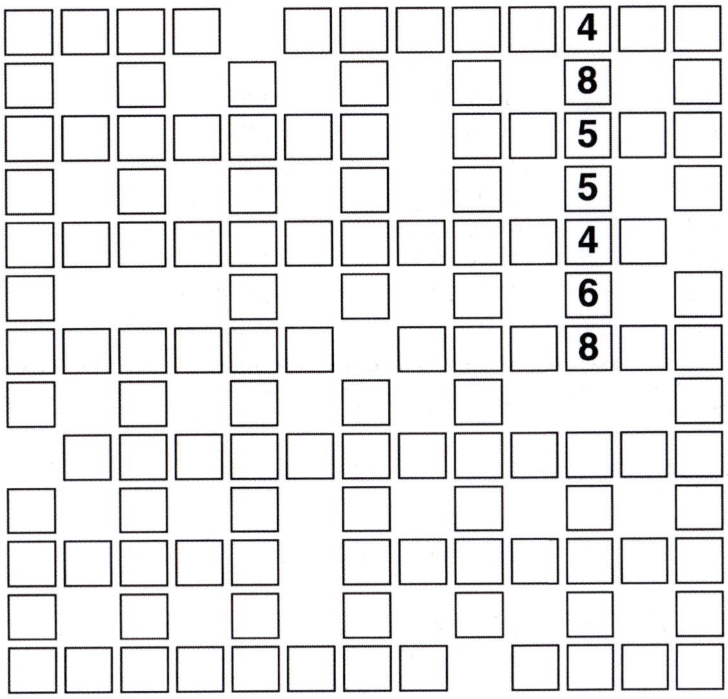

Anagrams

Rearrange the scrambled letters to form words relating to computers.

WISEBET
(CLUE: You'd find it online)

CITYUSER
(CLUE: Passwords help with this)

OWNTREK
(CLUE: Something made up of different people)

WORDFINDER

A word has been hidden in the letter grid on the right. Simply cross out any letter that appears more than once and the hidden word will reveal itself. Write it in the boxes below. If you'd like an added challenge, see if you can solve the puzzle in your head without crossing out any letters.

Y	U	Q	V	T
S	T	E	J	Q
Y	G	H	S	M
V	J	X	A	H
X	I	G	L	U

Spot the difference

These two pictures of a gaming arcade appear to be the same, but take a closer look. There are five stupendously hard-to-find differences. Can you spot them?

BIG DEBATE

Should you reduce your screen time?

Research suggests that too much might affect our friendships and studies.

SMARTPHONE SOCIETY

As of 2018, 95% of people aged 16–24 in the UK owned a smartphone, according to Ofcom, an organisation that oversees communications in the UK.

We see them everywhere: in cinemas and on laptops, phones, smartwatches, tablets and TVs. Screens are a crucial part of most people's lives. In *The Incredibles 2*, one of 2018's biggest films, the villainous Screenslaver hypnotises people and controls their minds through screens. Although not based on fact, the storyline does reflect real-life concerns about the dangers of screens and the amount of time we spend looking at them. A 2015 study found teenagers who spent an extra hour at a screen each day would, on average, drop a grade in two GCSE subjects. However, screens can be really helpful, too. They open up new worlds of information and entertainment, and allow us to connect with people wherever they are. Life in the 21st century relies on screens and digital technology in a way that hasn't been the case before, but should people try to reduce their screen time?

YES

- **Spending so much time on screen means less time for friends and family, and besides, interactions online just aren't the same as speaking, laughing and joking with somebody in person.**
- **It's unhealthy to spend hours staring at a screen; the time could be better spent exercising and playing outside. Research shows too much can even lead to mental-health problems and a lack of sleep.**
- **Studies have connected a lot of screen time with getting lower grades in exams. It's time to put our phones away.**

NO

- **Looking at a screen is an essential way of learning. The internet is full of information and there are lots of apps that offer a better understanding of the world, so spending time on screens can be useful and informative.**
- **Lots of people have friends and family who live abroad. Screens allow people to speak to people who may be elsewhere in the world.**
- **It's fun – screens are used to play video games, watch YouTube, catch up on TV and films and listen to music.**

WHAT DO YOU THINK?

How to...

Make selfie props

Your photos will be even more fun with these easy-to-make accessories.

What you need

- Pencil
- Sheets of card (in different colours)
- Scissors
- Strong glue or sticky tape
- Paper straws or wooden skewers

Instructions

First, draw out the shapes of your props onto the card using a pencil. Good shapes to start with include beards, bow ties, hats, lips, moustaches, spectacle frames and speech bubbles. If you don't feel confident enough to draw these freehand, ask an adult to help, or search for templates online. Once you've drawn one, cut it out and use it as your stencil to create as many more of that shape as you like. When you are happy with all of your newly cut shapes, place a blob of glue on the left- or right-hand side of each shape and fasten the straw or stick to it. If you are using sticky tape, put the straw or stick on top of the cardboard cut-out before laying a piece of tape on top to keep it in place.

Frames and backdrops

Making props is a great way to jazz up your self portraits or photos of family and friends. Why not take it a step further and create a funky background or a cool cardboard frame to make your snaps really stand out? Pick a wall that you're allowed to stick things to, and go wild. Depending on your theme, you could hang paper garlands, strips of crêpe paper or bits of string to which you can peg things, such as cards or pictures. For your photo-booth frame, all you need is a big piece of cardboard. Cut a square in the middle and decorate your border with dates, names, ribbons and flowers. The possibilities are endless!

DID YOU KNOW?

The first photographic self-portrait is thought to have been taken in 1839 by an amateur photographer called Robert Cornelius.

COOL RUNNINGS

This picture is of Roman Repilov – a luge rider. Luge, which is French for sled, is about far more than just lying down. The sleds can reach speeds of 90mph as they hurtle down icy tracks and are mainly controlled by the athlete's upper body. The athletes need to be strong, alert and fearless. They have no brakes and no protection other than a helmet.

SPORT

Who are the greatest underdogs of all time and what are the world's strangest sports? Read on to find out...

History's weirdest

Some seriously strange games are still being played today.

If you take time to stop and think about it, sports are strange. People run around, trying to accomplish odd physical tasks that often serve no real purpose – usually while being cheered on by thousands of spectators. Sports can even seem odd to sports fans; many people who love cricket, for example, can't see the point of American football. The world is filled with weird and wonderful sports – and history abounds with them.

Why did sports start in the first place?

For much of human history, sports have offered people an opportunity to practise two important – if not very pleasant – activities: hunting and fighting. Throwing a spear with great accuracy was a useful skill if you needed to skewer a wild boar for supper, and a talent at wrestling could come in handy for anyone expecting to spend time on a battlefield. In the past, people realised that they could have fun practising these skills – and prove their talent by competing against others in front of huge crowds.

SAME BUT DIFFERENT

The ancient Olympics had much in common with today's, but some things were very different. For one thing, athletes were expected to compete stark naked.

The Olympics

The winning French Olympic pistol-duelling team in 1908.

The Olympic Games is almost certainly the most famous sporting event in the world; 3.6 billion people tuned in to watch the Rio de Janeiro Games in Brazil in 2016. The Games originated 3,000 years ago, in ancient Greece, and were held in honour of Zeus, the Greek god of thunder and lightning. The modern Games began in 1896, but you might not recognise all of the sports. In 1906, pistol-duelling was an Olympic sport, although competitors shot at mannequins rather than each other. Rope climbing was also once an Olympic event; it began in 1896, and involved climbing to the top of a rope. Solo synchronised swimming was an Olympic sport between 1984 and 1992. It consisted of one person in the water, dancing to the music by themselves.

Still going strong...

Sports have come a long way since people were chucking around spears; nowadays, most are pretty far removed from war and survival. You don't have to look hard, however, to find that many of history's most bizarre sports are still very much alive.

A stoolball player.

Stoolball

Originating in England, stoolball is a game stretching back to the 15th century. It used to be popular all over the country and is mentioned in a play called *The Two Noble Kinsmen,* by William Shakespeare. Batsmen compete to score runs while bowlers and fielders try to get them out. Sound familiar?

and wildest sports

Buzkashi is wild and fast.

GRUFF GAME
Buzkashi is pronounced booz-ka-shee and means goat-pulling in Persian.

Spectacular sumo

No doubt you've have heard of sumo wrestling, but you might not believe how old the sport is. The Japanese have been staging sumo fights for at least 1,300 years – and probably much longer. Ancient paintings suggest sumo was a kind of prayer that was performed to try and bring a good harvest. The sport has remained more or less unchanged since the 1600s, and continues to draw impressive crowds who marvel as the giant wrestlers throw salt in the ring to get rid of evil spirits, before clashing like hulking bull elephants.

Calcio Fiorentino is a rough game.

Calcio Fiorentino

If you think some football teams play rough, you obviously haven't experienced Calcio Fiorentino. Also known as Florentine football, this sport comes from the Italian city of Florence, although it started in ancient Greece. The rules were officially published in 1580, and today's players still wear 16th century costumes. Two teams of 27 use a ball to score goals, but most of them just fight each other.

Buzkashi players.

Buzkashi

A stunning display of horsemanship, buzkashi is popular in Afghanistan, a country with a long history of mounted warriors. It dates back about 600 years, and was brought to Afghanistan by invading armies from the east. Competitors race their horses around the pitch to grab an object that they place in a goal to score points. The object isn't a ball, though – it's a dead goat or calf.

Snow business
Konstantin Andreev rides high with his bike as he performs tricks at Ladozhskoye Lake, Russia.

A clean getaway
A competitor dressed as cartoon character Obelix in a soapbox cart race in Rome, Italy.

Hand in the sand
Megumi Murakami, of Japan, takes a dive in the Beach Volleyball Major Series.

DID YOU KNOW?
Volleyball players once competed for 101 hours, claiming a record for the longest indoors contest in the sport.

Falling with style
Canadian Lysanne Richard at the Red Bull Diving World Series in Switzerland.

A STRANGE SPORT

In the 1904 Olympics, athletes competed in an odd sport: diving into a pool and gliding along without moving their bodies.

On the ball
A participant shows off his skills in a freestyle football contest in Chile.

An ice feeling
Angela Van Wiemeersch makes a perilous climb in Michigan, US.

SPORT'S GREATEST UNDERDOGS

All fans enjoy seeing the best sportsmen and women compete against each other, demonstrating the peak of sporting excellence, but it's often just as enjoyable when an unexpected victory occurs. Here are a few of the best upsets and most remarkable wins of all time.

Japan's unexpected triumph

South Africa have won the Rugby World Cup twice; Japan had won just one of their previous 24 World Cup matches going into the 2015 Rugby World Cup tournament. When the two teams met, no one expected Japan to keep up with South Africa, but with eight minutes to go, the score was 32-29 to South Africa. In the final seconds, Japan passed up the chance to kick a three-point penalty that would have ended the game in a draw and instead scored a winning try to seal a 34-32 win. Commentators said it was the biggest upset in rugby history. Japan's coach Eddie Jones, now England's head coach, said, "If you are a child in Japan you will watch this and you will want to play rugby for Japan in the next World Cup." Japan are hosting the Rugby World Cup in 2019.

Harumichi Tatekawa of Japan takes on Pat Lambie of South Africa.

DRAMATIC DEFEAT

In 1995, Japan lost in the highest-scoring Rugby World Cup game ever played. New Zealand won 145-17.

WOW! Sixty-six people joined together at Huntington Beach in California in 2015 to break the record for most people on one surfboard.

The shark-fighting surfer

Surfing is a difficult sport, requiring high levels of fitness, balance and bravery. Anyone who wins competitions is to be applauded, but some people have a harder time getting to the top. Bethany Hamilton from Hawaii, US, won her first national championship when she was 15. Two years earlier she had her left arm bitten off by a shark. Just the idea of getting back in the water would have put some people off, but Hamilton was surfing again just one month after the attack. Hamilton is still a professional surfer at the top level.

A trailblazer

Figure skating is a popular part of the Winter Olympics. UK skater Madge Cave Syers broke new ground in 1902 when she became the first woman to compete in the sport's world championships. Although only men had competed before, she realised that the rules made no mention that women weren't allowed to enter, so she took part – and came second. In 1906, she won the newly created women's world championship, and in 1908 she became the first woman to win an Olympic figure-skating gold medal.

The part-time tennis player

In 1976, Mark Edmondson, a part-time hospital cleaner from New South Wales, Australia, qualified for the prestigious Australian Open tennis tournament. Although he was ranked 212th in the world, he stunned tennis fans by getting all the way to the final where he faced fellow Australian John Newcombe. They had won a set each in the final when a strong wind disrupted the match and the umpire called a temporary halt. When they came back out Edmondson dominated and earned a legendary win... but dropped the trophy when he was presented with it.

Leicester City celebrate their fantastic win.

Lineker keeps his promise.

A bolt from the blue

Leicester City shocked the world when they became English Premier League champions in 2016. In the 20 Premier League seasons leading up to Leicester's big win, only Manchester United, Manchester City, Arsenal and Chelsea had won the title. Although the more famous clubs had spent more money on transfers and had better-known players, Leicester went top on 16 January and stayed there until the end of the season. Gary Lineker, a former Leicester player, said he would host TV show *Match of the Day* in his underwear if Leicester won the title – and he did just that in August 2016.

FAST FEET
Mo Farah wears his running trainers for an average of four weeks before replacing them with a new pair.

DOUBLE TROUBLE
Farah has a twin brother called Hassan, and twin daughters called Aisha and Amani.

Farah won two gold medals at the Rio 2016 Olympic Games.

Mo Farah races into the record books

As one of the world's most famous sportsmen, British athlete Mo Farah has enjoyed a glittering running career.

With four Olympic gold medals and six world titles in long-distance running, Mo Farah has had incredible success. Along with stars such as Jessica Ennis-Hill and Greg Rutherford, he shot to fame at the London 2012 Olympics by winning the 5,000- and 10,000-metre events. He won both titles again at the Rio Olympics in 2016. Farah retired from track running in 2017 to concentrate on road running and marathons, which are 26.2 miles long. He set a British record when he finished third at the 2018 London Marathon. Another (slightly more unusual) world record that Farah has set was for completing a 100-metre sack race in 39.91 seconds. If you've ever done the sack race in your school sports day, you'll know how hard that is!

On your marks...

Farah was born in Somalia in 1983. Because of trouble and fighting in the African country, he moved to London with his family when he was eight years old. He spoke very little English and had to quickly adapt to life in a new country. Farah was very keen on football when he was at school; he loved playing it and he supported Arsenal. It was Farah's PE teacher, Alan Watkinson, who spotted his running talent and convinced Farah to focus on athletics as his main sport.

Mobot man

It was at the 2012 London Olympics when Farah first performed his "Mobot" victory celebration, where he arches his arms onto the top of his head to make an M shape. Jamaican sprinter Usain Bolt copied the move after winning gold in the 4x100-metre relay in 2012. Farah has a Mobot logo on his running shoes and clothes, and there's also a funny song and video called *Do the Mobot,* in which Farah appears, which helped raise money for the Mo Farah Foundation charity. In August 2017, he even did the Mobot while standing on top of the highest capsule on the London Eye.

Still training hard

Even though he will no longer compete in long-distance running at the Olympics, Farah still trains and practises hard for marathons and other races. Sometimes he runs up to 135 miles in a week, which is about the same as running around an athletics track 543 times. Farah will often eat porridge, scrambled egg and toast for breakfast to give him energy for his training, and he likes meals with chicken and salmon to keep him fit and healthy. One of Farah's favourite meals to cook is spaghetti bolognese and he admits to having a sweet tooth and enjoying puddings.

Catching up with Mo

The Olympian tells *The Week Junior* what makes him tick.

The Mobot.

How do you stay motivated?
I'm really proud of what I achieved on the track. I recently moved from track running to the road marathon and I really believe that I can win medals on the roads too, so I'm determined to put in the hard work to achieve results. I broke the British record at the London Marathon this year and I'm aiming to compete at the Tokyo Olympics in 2020.

Who's the most famous person in your phone's contacts?
My good friend Usain Bolt is pretty famous around the world, so I'll say him!

What do you enjoy doing in your spare time?
I've got four kids and I absolutely adore spending time with them – especially as I'm away for several months of the year at training camps, so I miss them loads. I absolutely love football, so when I'm away training I'll watch a lot of football matches (I support Arsenal) and play a lot of FIFA.

Do you dream of playing for Arsenal one day?
Yeah, I love Arsenal. When I was younger, I really wanted to be a professional footballer – but the truth is I probably wasn't good enough to be pro. I do love to play whenever I can, though.

Famous face

Farah is often featured in magazines and on television shows; he played in the Soccer Aid celebrity charity football match for England in June 2018. The athlete also has his own YouTube channel, where he discusses running tips and secrets, and he's said that one day he'd like to appear in *EastEnders*, his favourite TV soap opera. On 31 December 2016, the Queen gave him the honour of being called a Sir and he was officially knighted at Buckingham Palace in November 2017. "Looking back at the boy who arrived here from Somalia, I could never have imagined where I would be today," he said, after receiving the award.

Wordsearch

Can you find all of these tennis terms in the grid? They may be hidden horizontally, vertically or diagonally, and reading either forwards or backwards.

ACE
ADVANTAGE
ANDY MURRAY
APPROACH SHOT
BACKHAND
BACKSPIN
BASELINE
CAROLINE WOZNIACKI
CHALLENGE
COURT
DAVIS CUP
DEUCE
DOUBLE FAULT
FIRST SERVE
FOREHAND
GRAND SLAM
GRIP
GROUNDSTROKE
JOHANNA KONTA
LINE JUDGE
MARIA SHARAPOVA
NOVAK DJOKOVIC
POINT
RAFAEL NADAL
RALLY
RANKINGS
ROGER FEDERER
SECOND SERVE
SERENA WILLIAMS
SERVE AND VOLLEY
SIMONA HALEP
SINGLES
SMASH
TIEBREAK
TOPSPIN
TRAMLINES
UMPIRE
VENUS WILLIAMS
WILD CARD
WIMBLEDON

A	D	V	A	N	T	A	G	E	F	I	R	S	T	S	E	R	V	E	A
S	E	R	E	N	A	W	I	L	L	I	A	M	S	F	C	T	D	E	N
E	C	A	E	G	D	U	J	E	N	I	L	S	R	I	N	N	G	B	D
J	J	O	H	A	N	N	A	K	O	N	T	A	V	I	A	N	A	R	Y
A	O	G	R	A	N	D	S	L	A	M	L	O	P	H	E	C	W	I	M
W	V	R	D	A	V	I	S	C	U	P	K	S	E	L	K	F	I	Z	U
Y	D	O	T	O	P	S	P	I	N	O	K	R	L	H	D	O	L	A	R
E	T	G	P	S	M	A	S	H	J	C	O	A	A	S	O	H	D	L	R
L	O	E	S	A	M	S	N	D	A	F	H	N	H	E	U	U	C	A	A
L	H	R	L	E	R	A	K	B	I	C	D	D	A	N	B	O	A	D	Y
O	S	F	I	K	C	A	I	N	Z	O	W	E	N	I	L	O	R	A	C
V	H	E	S	Q	V	O	H	L	N	S	S	D	O	L	E	I	D	N	T
D	C	D	G	O	R	U	N	S	L	O	A	L	M	M	F	R	S	L	N
N	A	E	N	R	B	P	H	D	A	I	D	G	I	A	A	A	E	E	Z
A	O	R	I	C	O	U	R	T	S	I	W	E	S	R	U	L	C	A	F
E	R	E	K	I	U	M	P	I	R	E	R	S	L	T	L	L	U	F	T
V	P	R	N	S	E	L	G	N	I	S	R	A	U	B	T	Y	E	A	T
R	P	T	A	T	I	E	B	R	E	A	K	V	M	N	M	A	D	R	L
E	A	G	R	I	P	B	A	S	E	L	I	N	E	E	E	I	H	I	J
S	I	E	K	O	R	T	S	D	N	U	O	R	G	A	P	V	W	T	M

ANSWERS CAN BE FOUND ON PAGES 94–97

Keyword crossword

Once you have completed the crossword, use the letters in the yellow boxes to spell out another word. Write the keyword in the boxes below the clues.

Across

3 Running competitions (5)
5 Not inside (7)
6 What singers create and perform (5)
8 Lift up (5)
10 Alike (7)
12 Delicate; easily broken (7)
13 Not smooth (5)
15 Animal of the camel family (5)
16 Aged between 13 and 19 (7)
17 Extra; not currently in use (5)

Down

1 Sad (9)
2 Seeks an answer (4)
3 Recall (8)
4 Windsor ___: one of the Queen's residences (6)
7 Acrobatic feat (9)
9 Guess (8)
11 Country in North America whose capital is Ottawa (6)
14 Sound a pig makes (4)

Keyword clue: Often a summer game.

Code riddles

These rugby words have had each letter replaced by the letter after it in the alphabet (so A becomes B, B becomes C and so on). Can you break the code to reveal the answers?

DPOWFSTJPO =

ESPQ HPBM =

QFOBMUZ USZ =

Number tower

Place a number in every square to complete the number tower. The value in each square is the sum of the numbers in the two squares directly beneath it.

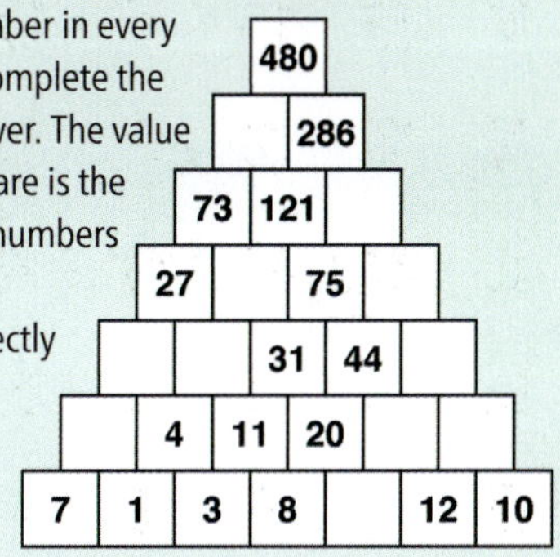

Spot the difference

These two pictures of the Tour de France might appear to be the same, but take a closer look. There are five fantastically hard-to-find differences. Can you spot them?

BIG DEBATE

Should children train to play professional sports?

Many of the world's top athletes have been training since they were young.

DID YOU KNOW? According to the National Health Service (NHS) young people should aim for at least 60 minutes of physical activity every day.

Sport plays a major role in society. There are many famous tournaments and events that are played all over the world, such as the Olympics and the football World Cup. Winners are often rewarded with money, fame and glory, but getting to the top is hard work. Some of today's most successful sportspeople started training at a young age. England footballer Harry Kane began training with Arsenal football club at eight, and Tom Daley, who dives for Britain, won his first medal at the same age. Superstar tennis player Serena Williams began playing when she was just three. Professional sports can be extremely intensive: by age 11, some elite swimmers are training as much as 27 hours a week, including early-morning sessions before school. Sport is thought to be very good for young people, but is this always the case when some clubs, coaches and parents are pushing them so hard?

YES

- **You have to start training at a young age if you want to be good enough to compete professionally in any sport.**
- **Sport is a positive way for young people to spend their time and it's much better than watching TV or playing computer games. It makes you fit and healthy.**
- **You'll learn skills you might not pick up at school, including discipline, teamwork and how to deal with success and failure.**
- **To get to the top of your game and travel around the world for tournaments is an incredible experience.**

NO

- **Training takes the fun out of sport. You miss out on hobbies and spending time with friends and family.**
- **Your schoolwork might suffer and it can be very tiring, too. A lot of pressure could result in emotional stress; children need time to relax and have fun.**
- **If you perform badly, you might get told off, which could affect your confidence, and you might feel guilty for letting down your coach or teammates.**
- **Even with training, you still might not be good enough to compete at the very top.**

WHAT DO YOU THINK?

How to...

Make energy-boosting bars

This no-bake bar will fuel all your sporting activities.

What you will need

- 340g oats
- 170g mixed nuts
- 170g mixed seeds
- ½ tsp cinnamon
- 170g peanut butter
- 60g honey
- 100g raisins
- 20cm square baking tray
- Greaseproof paper
- Food processor
- Spatula

Instructions

1. In a food processor, whizz together the oats, nuts, seeds and cinnamon. Just a few short pulses will mix the ingredients nicely.
2. Next, melt the peanut butter and honey in a bowl in the microwave for 30 seconds (make sure your bowl is microwave-safe) or in a saucepan on the hob, then add it to the oat mixture. Another few pulses in the food processor will combine the ingredients.
3. The mixture should stick together. If not, add another squirt of honey. Then stir in the raisins.
4. Tip the mixture into a baking tray lined with greaseproof paper and press down firmly with a spatula.
5. Put the tray in the fridge for two hours to set before cutting into 15 small bars. Wrap the bars in foil and keep them in the fridge until you are ready to eat them.

WARNING!
Ask an adult to help you when using a food processor, microwave or cooking on the hob.

NUTRITIOUS NUTS
Almonds contain vitamin E, which is good for your skin and eyes, and walnuts are rich in omega-3, a fatty acid that is good for your heart.

OATY GOODNESS
Oats contain something called fibre, which helps your digestion and makes you feel fuller for longer.

PROTEIN-PACKED
Peanuts are rich in protein, which you'll need if you like doing lots of sport.

How much can you remember?

1 In which country do most of the world's uncontacted tribes live?

2 What type of food was used to make the mortar that binds the stones of the Great Wall of China?

a) Noodles

b) Rice

c) Fish

a ☐ b ☐ c ☐

3 True or false? Nellie Bly travelled around the world in just 72 hours in 1889.

4 How many people in the world speak English?

a) 1.5 million

b) 1.5 billion

c) 1.5 trillion

a ☐ b ☐ c ☐

5 What is the most commonly forgotten item by people packing their bag, according to Amazon?

6 True or false? Cloud coverage is measured in units known as oktas.

7 How many words in spoken English was Koko the gorilla said to be able to understand?

a) Almost 1,000

b) Almost 2,000

c) Almost 3,000

a ☐ b ☐ c ☐

8 Jane Goodall is famous for studying which group of mammals?

2

12

16

9 True or false? Orcas are a species of whale.

10 The process of plants using the Sun's energy to grow is known as what?

a) Photosynthesis

b) Filmosynthesis

c) Picturesynthesis

a ☐ b ☐ c ☐

11 True or false? Coulrophobia is the fear of small spaces.

12 Who was the first person to set foot on the Moon?

a) Neil Armstrong

b) John F Kennedy

c) Buzz Aldrin

a ☐ b ☐ c ☐

13 Who wrote *A Brief History of Time*?

14 True or false? It's impossible to make a robot that can backflip.

15 Which of these do you not need to make a fizzy volcano?

a) A fizzy drink

b) A packet of Mentos

c) A Cornetto ice cream

a ☐ b ☐ c ☐

16 Which superhero does Dr Bruce Banner turn into?

17 True or false? Vincent van Gogh painted *The Starry Night*.

18 Who made the film *A Trip to the Moon*?

19 Which cinema snack is believed to have existed at least 5,000 years ago?

a) Doritos

b) Popcorn

c) Hot dogs

a ☐ b ☐ c ☐

20 True or false? A picture frame has been found that dates back 10,000 years.

21 When did the word emoji become an official part of the English language?

22 True or false? Mario first appeared as Jumpman in the game Donkey Kong.

23 On which machine did Ada Lovelace work?

a) The Academical Engine

b) The Astronomical Engine

c) The Analytical Engine

a ☐ b ☐ c ☐

24 In which 2018 film did the villain Screenslaver appear?

25 When was the first photographic self-portrait taken?

a) 1739

b) 1839

c) 1939

a ☐ b ☐ c ☐

26 True or false? The Olympic Games originated 3,000 years ago.

28

21

26

27 Which football team unexpectedly won the English Premier League in 2016?

28 Which of these records has Mo Farah not set?

a) A world record for the 100-metre sack race

b) A British record for the London Marathon

c) A world record for the 250-metre egg-and-spoon race

a ☐ b ☐ c ☐

29 True or false? Young people should aim for at least 15 minutes of physical activity every day.

30 What is omega-3?

a) A fatty acid

b) A secret spy boss

c) A military submarine

a ☐ b ☐ c ☐

CHECK YOUR ANSWERS

When you've answered all the questions, head to pages 96–97 to find out how many you got right.

WRITE YOUR SCORE HERE

/30

Answers

Around the world

Anagrams: rouble, pound, dollar
Keyword: America

O	C	O	M	O	R	O	S	A	A	N	A	H	G	E	M	E	T	S	T
I	I	M	A	U	R	I	T	A	N	I	A	T	K	L	O	E	Z	B	R
E	I	I	S	I	E	R	R	A	L	E	O	N	E	U	R	U	I	B	D
E	Q	E	A	N	A	W	S	T	O	B	Z	F	R	F	O	Q	D	E	X
A	Q	U	A	E	U	K	L	O	A	E	I	S	I	E	C	I	N	N	M
I	G	D	A	Y	T	A	E	R	A	A	M	E	T	G	C	B	U	I	A
L	R	A	K	T	I	H	U	N	I	I	B	Y	R	Y	O	M	R	N	D
A	S	H	M	B	O	G	I	W	Y	S	A	C	E	P	G	A	U	O	A
M	L	C	I	B	A	R	A	O	L	A	B	H	A	T	A	Z	B	S	G
O	A	M	T	N	I	L	I	L	P	A	W	E	J	T	B	O	Y	O	A
S	A	J	D	O	A	A	T	A	N	I	E	L	P	R	O	M	S	U	S
N	A	A	A	M	G	S	U	G	L	A	A	L	Z	X	N	E	T	T	C
C	Y	Z	L	S	V	O	O	R	A	G	K	E	D	A	N	A	S	H	A
A	B	V	G	R	A	L	B	R	W	R	U	S	A	E	M	A	V	S	R
M	I	S	E	S	A	R	I	Z	I	A	P	I	G	I	S	B	Q	U	L
E	L	G	R	H	G	B	J	U	I	J	N	A	N	Y	R	S	I	D	J
R	P	A	I	I	B	Y	D	O	A	R	L	D	I	E	S	E	Z	A	Q
O	O	S	A	F	A	N	I	K	R	U	B	W	A	Y	A	E	B	N	T
O	S	O	H	T	O	S	E	L	A	I	N	A	Z	N	A	T	P	I	O
N	R	A	I	S	I	N	U	T	D	O	N	I	G	E	R	I	A	S	L

■	A	L	T	H	O	U	G	H	■	■
■	■	O	■	A	■	N	■	O	■	■
E	G	Y	P	T	■	S	L	U	G	S
X	■	A	■	S	■	U	■	S	■	A
C	A	L	M	■	U	R	G	E	N	T
U	■	■	■	V	■	E	■	■	■	I
S	H	O	W	E	R	■	A	C	T	S
E	■	R	■	S	■	F	■	A	■	F
S	I	D	E	S	■	L	O	R	R	Y
■	■	E	■	E	■	E	■	O	■	■
■	■	R	E	L	I	A	B	L	E	■

Animals and environment

Code riddles: Persian, Siamese, Ragdoll
Anagrams: elephant, rhinoceros, leopard

T	Z	E	G	O	D	P	E	E	H	S	H	S	L	E	W	L	T	T	G
R	S	H	A	R	P	E	I	T	E	B	R	A	B	P	W	G	D	Z	C
P	E	A	E	S	H	I	H	T	Z	U	C	L	O	F	G	O	N	G	K
O	E	I	L	L	O	C	R	E	D	R	O	B	R	I	E	L	U	R	N
O	I	I	R	U	E	E	I	T	L	O	P	E	Z	G	N	D	O	Y	A
D	U	N	W	R	K	N	A	J	D	G	N	J	O	R	G	E	H	O	I
L	P	L	H	D	E	I	A	H	N	C	A	A	I	O	L	N	Y	R	N
E	Y	A	I	R	D	T	O	D	H	E	U	E	C	C	I	R	E	K	A
D	H	B	P	I	R	U	E	S	T	H	S	S	B	H	S	E	R	S	R
N	A	R	P	I	N	E	P	L	A	A	C	A	W	S	H	T	G	H	E
U	V	A	E	D	L	A	N	U	A	R	E	O	B	L	F	R	L	I	M
O	A	D	T	O	N	L	H	A	E	D	H	R	B	E	O	I	E	R	O
H	N	O	V	I	B	I	O	L	R	C	E	U	G	W	X	E	O	E	P
T	E	R	E	O	H	S	I	N	W	A	L	R	U	S	H	V	B	T	R
E	S	L	X	C	A	E	M	O	G	L	M	B	I	I	O	E	R	E	E
S	E	E	U	M	W	S	H	U	D	A	T	I	K	A	U	R	E	R	T
S	R	A	O	T	R	C	P	O	R	Q	B	T	E	N	N	S	O	R	N
A	D	Y	T	E	S	E	G	N	I	K	E	P	U	W	D	K	B	I	I
B	E	O	O	S	L	B	E	R	G	E	R	P	I	C	A	R	D	E	O
D	R	U	V	R	O	O	A	F	G	H	A	N	H	O	U	N	D	R	P

R	E	N	E	W	A	B	L	E				
	N									G		
R	E	C	Y	C	L	E				R		
	R						W	A	T	E	R	
	G			F		S				E		U
H	Y	D	R	O	C	A	R	B	O	N		N
		R		R		N						L
O	Z	O	N	E		C	L	I	M	A	T	E
X		U		S		T						A
Y		G		T		U			S			D
G		H			C	A	R	B	O	N		E
E		T				R			I			D
N						Y			L			

Science and technology

Code riddles: reaction, oxygen, chemical
Wordfinder: plant

Q	S	L	U	N	G	S	E	O	D	L	C	R	T	O	E	T	S	A	T
P	K	E	F	A	T	F	R	I	V	M	D	G	T	S	V	F	S	M	W
T	I	M	H	U	I	Z	G	L	B	G	N	R	K	P	S	T	U	C	Z
O	N	Y	E	L	R	E	R	H	E	N	A	E	P	R	O	S	A	A	L
N	C	Z	E	R	S	D	P	N	A	E	L	S	A	M	C	R	H	L	O
A	I	N	Y	T	R	G	E	G	H	E	L	E	A	L	B	X	S	T	C
A	Q	E	I	L	J	T	R	U	T	O	K	C	E	O	A	S	U	H	I
I	A	O	B	A	I	O	V	O	S	R	H	S	H	J	Y	T	G	G	H
P	N	D	R	C	E	V	N	S	R	N	N	Y	N	E	Z	N	N	I	C
A	Z	B	S	M	T	Z	E	R	E	L	D	X	N	C	H	A	U	S	U
A	I	R	E	T	C	A	B	R	W	R	A	D	Q	O	T	L	F	N	O
S	S	A	R	E	S	P	I	R	A	T	I	O	N	I	U	P	G	O	T
S	R	X	E	T	F	B	R	T	O	K	T	D	R	S	O	X	I	I	D
U	E	S	S	E	R	O	E	N	A	I	B	I	H	P	M	A	I	T	J
E	W	B	O	N	H	N	Q	A	P	S	S	Q	P	R	O	T	E	I	N
L	O	X	N	O	M	E	H	P	P	L	R	E	N	E	R	G	Y	R	B
C	L	T	W	M	U	S	F	H	L	A	N	I	M	A	L	S	O	T	R
U	F	T	S	R	T	B	R	E	A	T	H	I	N	G	A	T	S	U	A
N	I	T	U	O	D	U	C	G	F	P	S	M	E	L	L	G	I	N	I
A	J	T	O	H	A	Q	S	U	R	I	V	E	Y	E	S	W	U	H	N

	5	5	8	3	1	1	5	5	9	6	7	
1		8		6		8		5		5		1
1		9		1	7	9	0	4		4	9	2
6	4	3	7	2		2		6		8		8
5		7		0		6		1	6	0	5	3
8	7	5	7	6	1	8	8					2
4		4		1				1		1		2
4					4	3	0	0	8	3	4	2
2	3	2	8	7		0		1		3		1
4		8		2		1		7	9	8	1	1
8	4	3		3	4	3	7	6		0		4
6		6		5		6		4		8		4
	1	1	1	1	7	4	0	6	4	2	7	

1	5	6	4	2	3
3	2	4	6	1	5
2	3	1	5	4	6
4	6	5	1	3	2
6	4	2	3	5	1
5	1	3	2	6	4

478
209 269
86 123 146
36 50 73 73
19 17 33 40 33
14 5 12 21 19 14
12 2 3 9 12 7 7

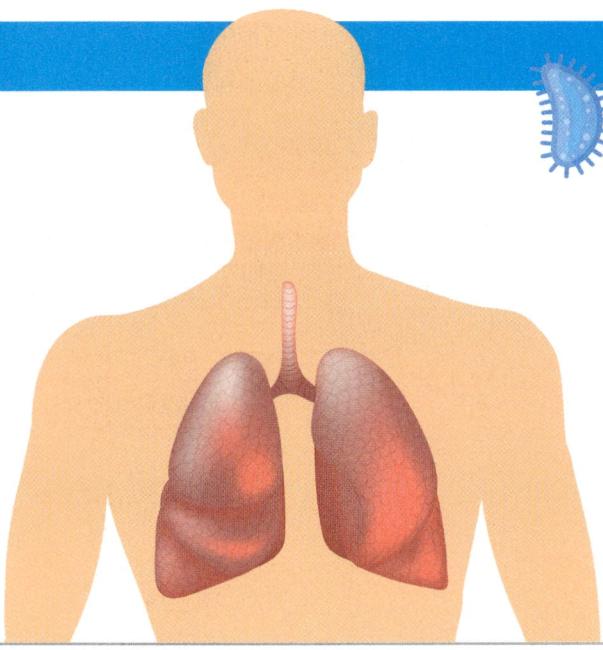

Arts and entertainment

Anagrams: illusionist, actor, acrobat
Keyword: comedian

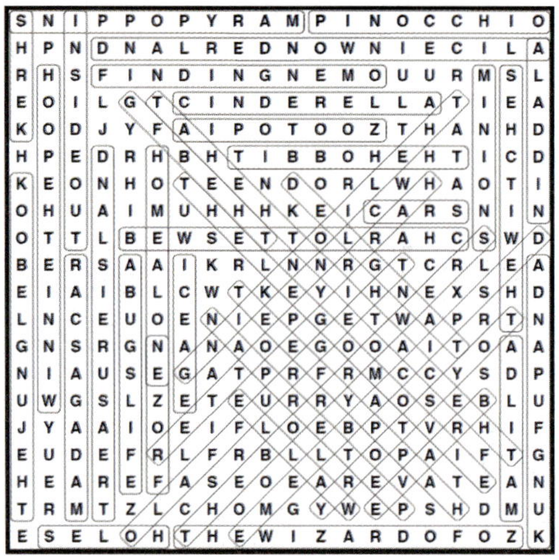

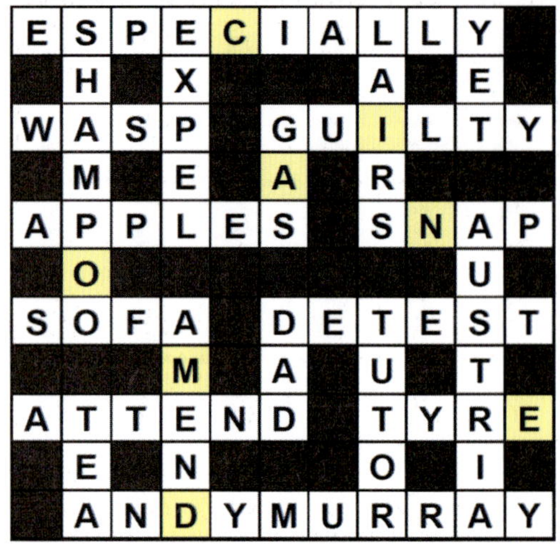

On screen

Anagrams: website, security, network
Wordfinder: email

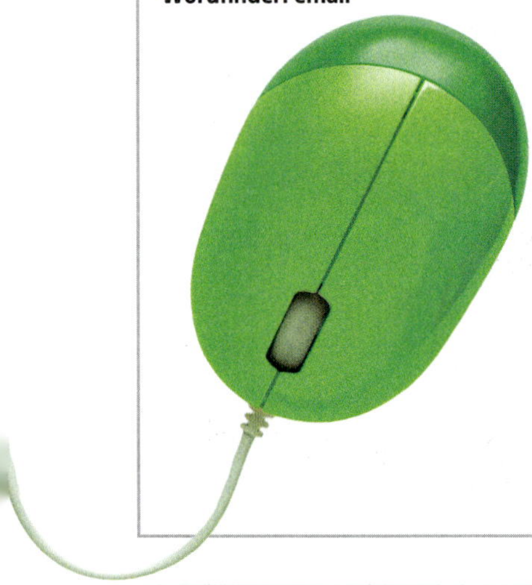

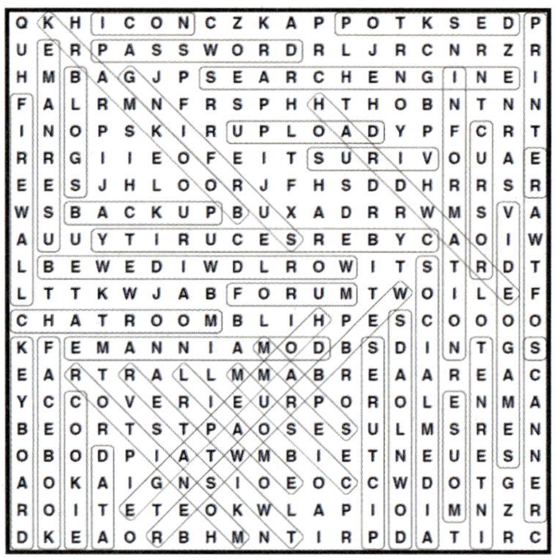

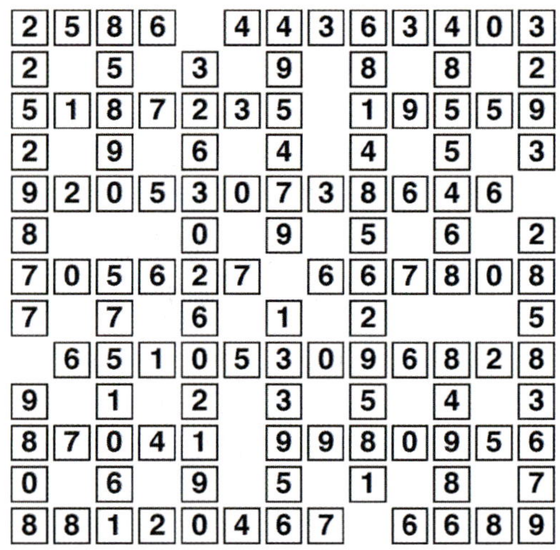

Sport

Code riddles: conversion, drop goal, penalty try
Keyword: cricket

Quiz answers **1** Brazil **2** b) Rice **3** False, it was 72 days **4** b) 1.5 billion **5** Phone charger **6** True **7** b) Almost 2,000 **8** Primates **9** False, they are a species of dolphin **10** a) Photosynthesis **11** False, it's the fear of clowns **12** a) Neil Armstrong **13** Stephen Hawking **14** False, backflipping robots have been invented **15** c) A Cornetto ice cream

6	1	2	4	3	5
5	3	4	2	1	6
3	2	6	1	5	4
1	4	5	3	6	2
2	5	3	6	4	1
4	6	1	5	2	3

480
194 286
73 121 165
27 46 75 90
12 15 31 44 46
8 4 11 20 24 22
7 1 3 8 12 12 10

16 The Hulk **17** True **18** Georges Méliès **19** b) Popcorn **20** False, the oldest dates back to the second century **21** 2015 **22** True **23** c) The Analytical Engine **24** *The Incredibles 2* **25** b) 1839 **26** True **27** Leicester City **28** c) A world record for the 250-metre egg-and-spoon race **29** False, it's 60 minutes **30** a) A fatty acid